Using
the
Power of Humor

Nothing helps
the battered spirit
more than laughter.

Using
the
Power of Humor

Forrest Wheeler

BestSeller Books
Wilsonville, Oregon

All proceeds of this book are donated to C.I.P. a nonprofit organization to promote humor.

Cover design by Richard Ferguson
Text design by Sheryl Mehary

BestSeller Books
Distributed by
Book Publishers Network
Bothell, Washington

Dedication

This book is dedicated to those who
seek joy and happiness
in their celebration of life.

Forrest Wheeler

Table of Contents

Author's Note

Using the Power of Humor is an easy and fun book to read. The practical applications of humor in every day life make this a permanent reference book as well as entertaining. This is a book that opens new and exciting ways to empower yourself by connecting humor to:

Health and Healing

Education and Learning

Increased Productivity

General Sense of Well Being

Additionally, this book will enable you to access laughter and humor in privacy, your daily activities and interaction with others.

Using the Power of Humor provides you with an easy to understand and usable definition of humor. It clearly separates humor from comedy. It demonstrates in simple language the appropriate from inappropriate uses of humor and comedy. In so doing it provides you with new perspectives on humor giving you permission to take humor seriously.

Also, the information in this resource will open up a whole new category of humor which the author identifies as irrational humor. The use of irrational humor when combined with rational and physical humor improves our understanding of clowns. It broadens the potential role clowns play as a positive influence in our community.

In a world filled with contradiction, anger, fear and guilt, *Using the Power of Humor* is a welcome alternative to finding fulfillment in our lives. The line between mendacity and ultimate reality is razor thin.

What About Your Author?

The author of this book is not supposed to exist. It was all a mistake. The mistake happened in 1933, when a twenty-year-old girl had sex with her seventeen-year-old cousin and I was the result. A failed attempt to "erase" this mistake was made by leaving me in a warm oven with the glass door closed. Had it not been for my grandmother who discovered me I would have smothered. I was left permanently brain damaged. My grandfather's suicide two years later did not help matters much. I grew up in an abusive dysfunctional household in which those responsible for me found my existence annoying. I was an outcast in my community, barely tolerated in school, and shunned. By the time I was eighteen I was so inflamed with rage that the only remaining question was how many people would I destroy on the way to prison and death?

It is now sixty years later. Fifty of these years I have spent married to the most wonderful angel God created. Not surprisingly, she retired after thirty-five years as a special education teacher. We have two children who are adults and successfully fulfilling their lives with humor and adventure.

I took my Masters Degree in Education Administration to the Far East where we worked with children from twenty-three different nationalities in elementary Joint Consulate schools. Upon retirement I became a clown volunteering in hospitals and throughout the community.

The details of how this all happened are more complicated than I can relate. The point is I saved my life when at the age of nineteen I learned that anger — like debt — grows bigger and uglier. Humor is like an inheritance — it creates power and opportunity. Some of the things humor can do for you include helping you to:

- Develop positive attitudes

- Make lasting relationships

- Distance yourself from problems with minimum risk

- Increase your productivity

- Strengthen your immune system

- Reduces pain

- Enhances communication

- Change

This book started as a resource for "Humor 'R Us" club members to access the power of humor between meetings. "Humor 'R Us" is the national organization devoted to spreading the message that humor heals and is a gift from one person to another to improve the quality of life. Those members of the club exposed to this book recognized that the secrets revealed are also valuable to any person who desires to enrich his or her life.

Introduction

*The human race has only one effective weapon
and that is laughter.*

also

*The human is the only animal who blushes, or
needs to.*

– Mark Twain

There I was in full clown costume and face, perched atop a large wooden crate containing 20 tons of emergency hospital and food supplies. The crate and I were roasting ever so slowly on a sweltering airport tarmac in Kabul Afghanistan waiting for clearance through the laborious process of foreign immigration.

It was May of 2002. Afghanistan had just come through ten years of civil strife and was crippled by extensive devastation from military action by foreign inter- vention, religious and civil strife. The people of Afghanistan were exhausted with little hope for immediate improvement. Their country fit ever so well the definition of "a shambles." However, our little group of three clowns was determined to complete a mission of mercy.

Danny Kollaja from Corpus Christi, Texas — "Beach" secretary for the Gesundheidt Foundation — and I were in Afghanistan to deliver 40 tons of medical and food supplies to three orphanages and a children's hospital. These life saving institutions could only survive if funded by private charity groups. Our supplies were collected by Dr. Patch Adams through the Gesundheidt Foundation which he founded as a result of the movie about his life and how he used the power of humor to heal. I was making sure that none of them disappeared. The shortage of condensed bulk food and medicine was so severe that decisive action had to be taken to protect these supplies from theft. By drawing attention to ourselves and our antics we hoped to keep our "protectors" entertained so they wouldn't wander away, leaving the supplies unguarded.

The situation was extremely dangerous. The three of us were "foreign infidels" in a strict Muslim country that regarded many U. S. citizens as part of the occupation forces. In addition, I was a clown in a country whose closest word for clown was the English equivalent of "alien trickster". There I sat, red nose and all, attempting to entertain some forty-odd workers and eight youths assigned by the government of Afghanistan to keep us safe and to prevent the valuable supplies from disappearing into the thriving black market. Our position was disconcerting. Our protectors had little schooling, and precious little tolerance for western culture. Adding to our tension was the fact that these young men were armed with automatic rifles, which didn't exactly inspire us to relax. I was fully aware that any innocent provocation might result in Danny, Beach and me being shot. Leaning toward caution, I began to make balloon animals with slow, predictable movements.

Suddenly, I heard loud and boisterous laughter. Looking up, I saw Beach with an open tube of lipstick in her hand, chasing after an Afghan soldier. She was yelling "Bini! Bini!" (meaning "nose" in Afghani). My first thought is "That's it! We're all going to die."

An Afghani major, along with two of his army captains, emerged from their office and ran over to see what all the commotion was about. Beach was still laughing as she changed direction and went after the officers, trying to apply red lipstick on their noses. I started to wonder which fate would be preferable: dead from a bullet or dying of dehydration in a jail cell. My outlook did not improve when Beach still in hot pursuit with red lipstick extended, was concentrating on the commanding officer who was running away from her in full view of his subordinates. To my amazement, everyone was laughing.

Another officer stepped forward, pointed to his nose and taunted the clown to chase him. The game of tag continued for several minutes. When another officer came up to me and shook my hand, he said, "Bini," pointing to his nose. "Bini," I replied, pointing to my own. He invited my interpreter and me into his office for tea and conversation. During our visit he confided, "Our morale is very low. We've lost our will to laugh." Later he added, "You've enabled us to laugh again. On behalf of my men, I thank you."

Back at our shelter that evening, we excitedly discussed the events of the day. Our combined testimony concluded that the power of humor had transformed a tense situation, rife with possibilities of misunderstanding and even death, into one where cultural differences were bridged. As it turned out, lasting friendships were also forged.

Many challenges lay ahead, but an important conclusion of our arduous, three-week mission to Afghanistan was that a high-ranking Afghani army officer who had been present on that hot tarmac in Kabul, went to great lengths to ensure that all 20 tons of our emergency supplies arrived safe and intact at their destinations. So, you tell me; do you think humor and laughter are powerful tools? On this occasion they proved to successfully complement all the resources of the United State's diplomatic and military arsenals combined.

Forrest "Muggins" Wheeler coaxes laughter from a shy Afghan girl who is forbidden to speak to foreigners.

Chapter One

How Do I Humor Thee? Let Me Count the Ways.

"Is there something wrong with with this picture?"

Like building a house, Chapter 1 lays the foundation for the rest of the book. This chapter provides you with:

1. A clear crisp definition of humor.

2. Three easy to apply categories of humor.

3. Separation of humor from comedy.

4. The practical application of different forms of humor.

Chapter One

How Do I Humor Thee? Let Me Count the Ways.

Humor is the absence of terror, and terror the absence of humor.

– Lord Richard Buckley

The practical application of different types of humor certainly was demonstrated in our Afghanistan experience. Here was a country that had suffered nine years of civil war and five years of drought. Everyone I talked to witnessed personal tragedy and death. Afghanistan is not the backdrop for humor and comedy. The mystery is why we were not killed. We were infidels. Our behavior could easily insult and demean the authority of military officers. Our costumes and makeup were irrational. Still I raise the question: Why were we not killed?

If we step back and take a second look at our experience in Afghanistan, something very powerful was happening. Beach serving as a clown jester or buffoon was a modern replica of jesters who have been around the Middle East for thousands of years. In the court of Pharaoh Dadkeri-Assi of Egypt some 4000 years ago, there was, a pygmy who acted as a court jester. To the east in China, during the Shang Dynasty (about 1818 B.C.), clowns were commonly seen around the Imperial Palace. Jesters and court fools had permission to laugh, play foolish jokes and games which violated tradition and rules of conduct. Regardless of tradition, time or geography, humans have regarded humor as a highly valuable asset to make us feel good, function well and cope with difficulties.

Our buffoonery in Afghanistan taught me two things. First the power of humor is great, and second, the line between the laughter and tears is razor thin. In our techno-logical world, we appear to have a love/hate relationship with humor. Television commentators are almost apologetic when they use humor — as if humor is a sign of immaturity. I have talked to many humorists and clowns who say they are often regarded as socially inept, politically naive or just plain silly. In reality, they are highly educated and extremely serious people who have the ability to make fun of themselves and to see the humor in life and creation.

It does not take a rocket scientist to know that little children laugh more often than adults. What happens between the backyard playpen and Junior High School? From an early age, we are taught that success in life requires a serious, mature outlook. The stern look and pointed finger from that giant called "Adult" selectively compromises our right to laugh. This is because the education of our children is structured and competitive. To be the best and come out "first" is the goal. Our educational systems focus most of their energy on the "top achievers" in the class. Life becomes bitterly serious and competitive in this modern scientific society. Have we lost the compassion and co-operative nature our ancestors held as precious? Have we lost the skill of using humor as a tool to soften the pain and risk of failure?

I remember the depression of the 1930s, the sacrifices we endured during WWII and the threat of a nuclear invasion during the 1950s. During the Great Depression, the extended family of aunts, uncles, nephews, nieces and cousins bonded together, sharing what little they had just to survive. This family solidarity carried over through WWII as many mourned the death of sons and daughters. But during these times there were always one or two family members who were great story-tellers.

Radio provided a grand source of humor through such programs as Amos and Andy, One Man's Family, The Dagwood Bumstead Program, Allan's Alley, It Pays to be Ignorant, Fibber McGee and Molly and Baby Snooks. The contributions kept our spirits with comedy. Humor kept us confident that better days were ahead and the war would soon end.

In the 1950s the new medium of television reflected a subtle change. Edward R. Murrow initiated a new kind of news broadcast that brought tragedy and terror into our living rooms. Soap operas, dramatizing the daily problems and fears of all Americans proliferated. Old traditional comedy such as the Jack Benny program, Bob Hope and Bing Crosby still lingered. But the sponsors sensed the public shift from humor to fascination with stories that exemplified the fears of viewers.

Although the 1950s were years of prosperity and growth, scars from the recent past made themselves felt. As my Uncle Bud put it; "My children will never suffer the way I did!" Commercials echoed this statement with constantly updated products that changed "wants" to "needs". Americans deserved a better life was the rationale, and manufacturers produced everything that might fulfill our fantasies. Humor began to change. Humor with a strong moral message appeared to diminish. In its place came the "comic". Comics of the 1950s and 1960s saw the emerging trends of conspicuous consumption, the growth of the feminist movement, the desire of people to be free to be themselves and to develop their own potential. The children from these years learned well.

"I will not be denied" was a growing trend of thought. As youth competed for identity and success, they also sought to escape the pressures to achieve.

Media humor was identified with the employee who was also a drunk, the inept and inefficient teacher or politician. We began to lose confidence in our neighbors, members of our family and the established institutions of our society. Moralistic humor was seen as "humbug". We wanted humor like "Our Miss Brooks," that portrayed teachers as vulnerable and prone to mistakes as we saw ourselves in our daily lives..

Then a peculiar thing happened. During the last quarter of the 20th century, science and technology exploded. One of the discoveries was that humor plays a vital part in our very survival. Dr. William Fry at Stanford University was able to prove that humor reduces stress, boosts immunity, relieves pain, decreases anxiety, stabilizes moods, enhances communication, inspires creativity and bolsters morale. His research showed that humor can help us cope effectively in these challenging times of rapid change and increasing complexity. Humor, it seems, helps us to communicate, mend relationships, resolve disputes and just plain feel better, it has received the backing of extensive scientific research. There exists widespread evidence that humor evokes emotions of sympathy, optimism, a positive outlook, generosity, responsiveness, compassion, kindliness, interest, understanding, consideration and acceptance. What a wonderful arsenal of tools for life in the Twenty-First Century!

Now, of all times, we need to enrich ourselves with the skills of humor. Millions of baby boomers are facing retirement. Some are accepting the "golden handshake", others are like Tom.

Tom was a tenacious, competitive, hard-working businessman, who for thirty years ran a neighborhood hardware store. At the age of 58, poor health forced him to sell his business. His routine became one of turning on the television, pouring a bowl of chips, opening a can of beer and spending the day in his favorite chair. His friend Don came by to see how he was doing. He found his friend gaining weight, with an ashen complexion and a very bad attitude.

Don invited Tom to accompany him to visit a thirteen-year-old boy in the hospital, who was scheduled for surgery the next morning. Reluctantly, Tom accepted the invitation. They stopped by Don's house on the way to the hospital. As Tom drank coffee, Don disappeared. What emerged minutes later gave Tom a shock; Don was now "Dr. Hick-Up," a hospital clown. Don's costume was composed of an oversized stethoscope, a CD disk strapped to his orange wig, a white doctor's coat with humorous buttons, oversized shoes and complete clown make-up.

"Have you gone crazy?" Tom asked, "You look absolutely ridiculous! How is a thirteen-year-old going to react to your crazy outfit?"

"We'll see," Don said.

The two men arrived at the hospital's prosthetic ward where an ice cream party had been prepared. Tom helped to serve ice cream while he watched his friend do magic tricks and talk to patients. He paid special attention to Robert, the thirteen-year-old boy who had been active in junior high athletics. Robert was to have his leg amputated the next morning. The boy was glum and bitter. Don challenged the boy to a game of "hangman". During the entire game, "Dr. Hick-Up" peppered the boy with all kinds of riddles, puns and knock-knock jokes. By the time he was finished, the boy was smiling and had finished off two servings of ice cream.

On the way back to Tom's house, a thoughtful silence enveloped the two men. As they pulled to a stop, Tom asked, "How can I get involved?"

Two months later, Tom and Don were sharing "Hospital Clown" experiences. Tom learned that bringing joy and happiness into the hearts of patients brought him great rewards. He regained his feeling of self-worth, developed a keen sense of humor and made many new friends. The hospital nutritionist taught Tom better eating habits and he lost his unwanted weight. Tom developed a healthy, positive outlook towards the future. Humor, and sharing with those who desperately needed it, changed Tom's life from quiet desperation to joyous anticipation.

You don't have to go to a foreign country to use humor for building bridges between people. There are endless opportunities in everyday life. Here's an example where humor helped develop a better rapport between two different age groups, easing the distance between two individuals: A six-year-old boy asked his grandfather, "How old are you Gramps?"

"I am 78 years old," the old man replied. Awed, the boy asked, "Gosh, is that starting with number one?"

The grandfather viewed seventy-eight years as old. The child contemplated it merely as a series of numbers. The boy's innocent remark bridged the distance between these two individuals by creating spontaneous humor and the opportunity to develop a deeper friendship through shared humor.

Humor is a powerful tool to improve productivity. This is evident in the area of sales. Ernie wanted to become the best salesperson in his firm. He joined Toastmasters International. The organization helped him to practice structuring material, as well as learn to be a good listener. Toastmasters gave Ernie an opportunity to practice his humor on an informed audience. Ernie learned to think funny in order to be funny. He learned that possessing a sense of humor allows one to exude an aura of success. This aura comes across as sincere concern for others, as well as a sense of inner peace and security, which in turn inspires confidence in others. Far more than an ability to accumulate wealth, fame or rank, success in life requires the ability to see humor in day-to-day experiences. This is especially true in politics. Will Rogers, with his Oklahoma coyboy humor tickled a nation with his puckish jibes at politicians in the depression years, giving audiences a lift by making fun of a common enemy — the pols.

Ever notice how popular politicians are when they have the ability to seize a moment and spontaneously create laughter? Humor makes them seem more trustworthy, human and approachable. Our instincts are engaged because we tend to more readily trust people who make us laugh. Sharing laughter creates a sense of bonding and connecting, camaraderie and shared perspectives.

Humor comprises, and is inseparable from, many of life's experiences. As such, it's one of the most important qualities to cultivate. *Let's say a husband and wife are arguing. The husband finally says, "Okay. Why don't you just write out all the things I do that irritate you, and I'll work on them." A few weeks go by and the husband asks his spouse, "Whatever happened to that list of things I do that irritate you?" The wife responded cleverly by saying, "I need more time. I'm only up to the letter H."* In this case, humor reduced feelings of anger through a lighthearted overstatement of a problem that diffused the argument.

I've met people who have taken the power of humor to transform their lives from despair to never-ending joy. One of these persons was Mary. Mary was a 48-year-old single mother who spent eight hours a day, five days a week, month after month in front of a computer terminal. Her daughter had committed suicide and her son was in drug rehabilitation. For recreation, Mary watched television and visited with a few close friends. Particularly sad was the fact that Mary was a creative person. One day, a friend suggested she take up fashion design as a hobby and as a way to make extra money.

Mary became a skilled tailor. One day, she received an order for some clown costumes. She noticed that being around these humorous, joking and silly clowns was affecting her life. Her own sense of humor began to blossom. She found that she really loved to be among the clowns, for they brought joy and laughter to so many.

Finally, she quit her day job and added selling clown cosmetics to supplement her costume-making. Later she developed clown presentations on safety, environment and reading programs for schools. She soon became quite popular and spent most of her time spreading laughter. Mary just happened to stumble into a form of humor which matched perfectly with her creative skills and which eventually led to major changes in her life.

What happened to Mary and Tom are the kinds of things that occur when we are willing to take the risk of letting humor become part of our lives. In all walks of life, and for all kinds of people, the power of humor is pervasive and persuasive. The more understanding we have of humor and the more types of humor we understand, the more control we have over our lives and those with whom we come in contact. Luckily, humor is a skill that is available to all of us.

The ability to harness and control humor is the ability to control the quality of your life.

A Matter of Perspective

Not too long ago, I was looking at the movie "Airplane I". It is a great movie because it includes all kinds of humor. In one scene a woman starts laughing hysterically and a nun comes up and begins slapping her. Behind the nun is a line of passengers waiting to slap the hysterical woman in turn. Of course, plane crashes, panic and striking people aren't intrinsically funny; we know that the line between tears of joy and tears of sadness is slim. Perhaps this is because the acts of laughing and crying release tension from conflicting emotions. We know that laughing (or crying) may result when emotions are in conflict with each other. Does humor enable us to release tension in acceptable ways that other people may want to share?

Psychologists say the ability to find a humorous perspective in seemingly non-humorous scenarios is a uniquely human ability. I am convinced that my dog Hunter gets pleasure watching gray squirrels chase each other around the backyard feeder. He appears to dream up various ways to pounce on and destroy the little creatures, it becomes clear that pleasure is part of the overall mammalian experience. Pleasure and humor are not limited to humans. Yet humans appear to be the only creatures who laugh as an association with pleasure. Perhaps it's the survival mechanism nature gave us to help us deal with the stresses of a complex brain. In any case, humans are lucky. We have the ability to find humor in subtle mistakes. *We can consciously choose to find humorous perspectives in situations that might otherwise appear to be non-humorous.* For example, a child crawls up on a couch to nestle against his grandfather. "Grandpa, would you make a sound like a frog?" he asks.

"Why do you want me to do that?" questions his grandfather.

"Well," the boy says, "Dad says that we'll get a lot of money when you croak."

The choice to find a humorous perspective from his grandson's innocent remark, or to feel hurt by his son's lack of tact, was up to the older man. Which choice do you think would be the most pleasant and help Grandfather live longer? He who laughs — lasts.

Going back to the benefits to be obtained from a movie like "Airplane I" provides a whole series of situations that are both frustrating and confusing. Those involved in the story and those in the audience find emotional release by choosing to see the story from a humorous perspective. The movie is full of contradictions, irony and choices. Choices to find humor in our own day-to-day experiences. You drive up to your neighborhood service station to discover that the price of gas has increased. Curious, maybe concerned, you learn that the reason gas prices are higher is because it is summer. People are driving more than usual on their vacations, so the demand for gas has increased. In another season, you drive up to your local service station to discover that the price of gas has again dramatically increased. This time, you learn that the increase is not because of higher demand, but because of a gas shortage. It doesn't take a lot of thought to realize that there is a serious contradiction in "logic" between the two prices. You may not be able to do anything about the increase in gas prices, or the questionable excuses to explain it, but you can choose to find the humor in the contradictions in order to ease your frustration. The opportunities are many for humor or to laugh and poke fun at deceptive practices of oil companies. The choice of perception is yours.

Church, state and corporate institutions provide wonderful occasions for humor as they reveal our contradictions and hypocrisy. For example: a minister compiles a list of 750 sinful acts. Within a week of announcing this, 200 of his parishioners have requested a copy. Is this hypocrisy? If hypocrisy is not acceptable — it is humor. If not an acceptable mistake, it may lead to frustration and anger.

Advertisements provide ample examples of hypocrisy. From automobile manufacturers that suggest their car provides sex appeal to stores that boast an item is free.The urge to misrepresent is often comical because it doesn't fool anybody and reveals the chicanery in the messages. If you go to purchase the free item, you discover it is only available when you purchase a certain amount or three other of the exact same items. The contradiction between the advertising and the purchase becomes comical because humorists use these events as fodder to reveal the cynicism behind the advertising strategy. Politicians who promise more and more benefits without increasing taxes, contradict any notion of common sense. Hypocrisy is all around us. But it can be called to account through humor which is a two-edged sword that makes fun and identifies those who try to cheat us. Few cynics can stand the bright light of humor.

The above are just a few examples of how humans can find curative humor in the peculiarities of the human condition. Politics, corporate institutions, churches and schools are going to continue to provide us with mistakes that promote humor. While we can not change these institutions, humor provides relief by allowing us to distance ourselves from the tension these contradictions create. Accessing the power of humor opens the opportunity to discovery and creativity. Discovery and creativity empowers us to deal with frustration and tension.

Nothing is funny in and of itself. It is our perspective that creates the experience of humor, and that's good news, because our perceptions are emotions which we can work with and change. Scientists have confirmed that humor is physically and emotionally good for us.

How does perception determine what is humorous to us? Well, what if someone slips and falls and we laugh. If it's apparent the person who fell is hurt, it ceases to be funny. Very clever and talented comics have been known to make us laugh at sensitive situations. In Erma Bombeck's At Wit's End, her lament on the problem of swimming-suit season provides a good illustration.

"No, I don't think I'm ready for a bikini again this year. Heaven knows I try to bend to the dictates of fashion, but let's face it; I'm a loser. When I grew my own bustle, they went out of style. When my hips reached saddlebag proportions, the "long, lean look" came in. When I ultimately discovered a waistline, the straight skirt came into being. I had a few, bright moments when they were exploring the flat chest as denoting women with high I.Q.'s, but then someone revealed a certain, clearly un-flat movie star's 135 (I.Q., that is) and shot that theory down."

"Tell you what, if I don't shape up by June, go on to the beach without me. Stop on the way back and I'll serve you a dish of homemade shortcake, topped with fresh strawberries, crusted with powdered sugar and wallowing in a soft mound of freshly whipped cream."

What's funny to one person may not be funny to another. Take this riddle: *"Question: What did one shoe say to the other shoe?" Answer: "Nothing. You couldn't talk either if your tongue was tied."* Such silly little nonsense may be riotous to a child, but would probably fall more into the "ho-hum" category for an adult. Likewise, cultural peculiarities can dictate what's found to be humorous or not. British transit system jokes are funny to people living in London while the rest of the world doesn't get the humor. Humorous anecdotes in the U.S.A. about the western frontier might get deadpan reactions in London. Humor is one of the last frontiers to cross when it comes to understanding a different culture. Age, sex and culture are also things that can determine our ability to find a situation humorous. What is humorous to many men might not be humorous to women. What the elderly find humorous might seem "dumb" to a youth. What is funny to black Americans may be lost to white Americans and vice-versa.

While humor varies according to age, sex, and cultural background, it remains a powerful force. To access this force and apply it to our lives is the purpose of this book. If humor is the result of humans dealing with harmless "mistakes" then our skill at controlling how we perceive these mistakes determines our ability to use humor to our advantage. One of the keys of cultivating our ability to find more humor in life is to practice distancing ourselves from our ego's investment in "self-image." If I make a mistake, but am fearful and cannot distance myself, my reaction is usually one of embarrassment or anger. If I make the same "mistake," but can take a moment to distance myself from my investment in self-image, I can more readily find the humor. I thus open the door to solutions or responses that I might not otherwise be able to see.

Once I was performing before an audience of about 300 people made up of all ages and backgrounds. To my horror, a teenager began heckling me. "You're not a real clown!" he teased, "I know how you do that trick!" he shouted. He put me in an awful position; if I argued with him, I would lose the rest of my audience. I tried ignoring him, but that didn't work. In desperation, I called for a volunteer from the audience to serve as my "Assistant Clown." Of course, this teenager vigorously raised his hand. I pretended not to see him, then finally turned and chose him as my assistant. This was risky. Having him join me on stage was an invitation for him to undermine my perform-ance territory. There was a possibility that he would damage my performance or access my props. Trying to maintain my objectivity, I put him to work helping round up other volun-teers from the audience, putting away used materials and generally helping with crowd control. The strategy worked. He was too busy helping me and too busy enjoying being my assistant to cause any further trouble. At the end of the performance, I had him take a big bow and receive a loud ovation from the audience. By distancing myself from my performer's ego, I was able to take a different perspective. This new view helped me to make the decision to include, rather than exclude, the heckler. How subtle, but great, is the power of humor.

Is it Humor or Comedy?

My son and I play golf. He is good and constantly self improving. I am horrid but love the game. We are like "Mutt and Jeff". He is on the fairway, I am in the rough. He keeps score, I could care less. Another set of players came up from behind us. We offered to let them play through. They said; "Naw, we can play along with you as a set of four."

Then I stepped up to hit the ball. "When they saw my stance, the two player simultaneously agreed to take up my suggestion to play through. My son and I thought that was very humorous. Later, my son said; "Dad how many narcissists does it take to change a light bulb?" "How many," I asked? "Only one, but he has to wait for the world to revolve around him."

While humor and comedy are enjoyed at the pleasure of the listener, there is a difference between humor and comedy. Humor is spontaneous and active. In this case it developed out of the experiences between four golf players. Comedy is a pre-rehearsed, performing art. In this case it was my son's "light bulb" joke. Comedy is a performing art that requires training, talent and a lot of hard work in order to be successful. Comedy, in the forms of cartoons, circuses, movies and live performances, are things we enjoy passively. The comedian consciously and deliberately creates the humor, and we vicariously enjoy the finished work of comedy.

The differences between "humor" and "comedy" are clear: we actively create "humor," while with "comedy," we are spectators. While this may seem a bit like splitting hairs to you, it's important to understand the difference between comedy and humor because, with a deeper understanding of the nature of humor, we are better able to incorporate humor in order to use its power to improve the quality of our lives.

What makes humor different from comedy is that humor is spontaneous and immediately enjoyed in our presence. Humor may involve conversation, but the conversation is frequently the very source of the humor. One of the reasons it's important to understand the difference between comedy and humor is that, while having a conversation, if you find the atmosphere becoming "tense," you can consciously use spontaneous humor to defuse it. However, if you tell a "pre-planned" joke to relieve social tension, you run the risk of appearing forced or artificial.

Is a joke humor or comedy? The following is an example of how "conversational" humor can deflect an otherwise embarrassing moment: In Singapore, the British and Chinese were attending a conference on economic development of Southeast Asia. A Brit, feeling awkward about the silence of the Chinese man to his left, leaned over smiling and asked, "You lika the soupee?" His companion simply gave a polite smile and remained silent.

Later, it turned out that this same man was the keynote speaker who spoke (in English) on the topic of economic trends. When he returned to his seat next to the Brit, he leaned over and asked, "You lika the speechee?" In this case, the story shows the active quality of humor turning a social "mistake" into an opportunity for insight about the error of cultural stereotyping. If this same situation were introduced as, "Have you heard about the Brit and the Chinese man?" Then the story would be comedy because the purpose of the humor is to entertain. All comedy must contain humor; humor does not have to be comical.

People who study different languages have concluded that the more important a subject, the more words are used to describe it. The Eskimos have several words for snow and we have several words for automobile. Likewise, humor and comedy is such an integral part of our human experience that we have, over the centuries, created all kinds of definitions and categories. There is contradiction, deviation, absurdity, pun, slapstick, physical, aesthetic, allegory, nonsense, ambiguity, circulatory, exaggeration, irony, mimic, simile, tricks, riddles, understatement, farfetched, free association, antithesis, incongruity, fallacies and many more. The result is a massive technology supporting the study of both comedy and humor. While this is good for academia, it does not deepen our understanding of how humor and comedy empowers us to improve the quality of our lives.

However, having a basic understanding of the kinds of humor and comedy is like having a toolbox or appliance cabinet. You cannot select a tool to solve a problem if you have no tools. Knowing the few basic kinds of humor enables us to easily apply humor and comedy to our lives. I have simplified all these categories and definitions into three basic simple parts. They are (1) Physical Humor (2) Rational Humor (3) Irrational Humor. To better understand these three categories, the use of the word humor also includes the idea of comedy.

1. Physical Humor

Two clowns, one in green and one in pink, are standing at a bus stop. A third clown, dressed in yellow, walks through carrying a long, flat board of wood. The clown in green shouts, "Watch where you're going with that plank!" The clown in yellow, carrying the plank, turns around quickly to see who is doing the shouting. The plank swings around with him. The clown in green who shouted sees the plank swinging towards him and ducks. The pink clown at the bus stop is smacked across the back and rolls across the ground. The clown in yellow, carrying the plank, turns to see what has happened as the clown in green reaches down to pull up his friend. This time, the plank catches the green clown across the rear, sending him sprawling on top of the pink clown already on the ground. The two struck clowns lying on the ground, then jump up and chase away the clown with the plank.

Physical comedy is any kind of "acceptable mistake" that focuses on physical activity — falling, tripping, mime, pantomime or slapstick. Clowns in circuses use physical comedy and humor with exaggerated gestures to communicate to an audience too large or far away to hear. Circus clowns perform with enormous props. They're blown out of cannons, explode out of refrigerators or fall off horses. A huge clown might step into a box marked "Washing Machine" and step out as a midget.

Physical humor of this nature is often as disciplined and physically demanding as ballet. I once went to the "Carumpa Circus" in Spain and saw a clown was rolling his hat down his arm, around his shoulder and down his other arm. I watched him for several minutes before going on to my conference. Emerging some two hours later, I saw him doing exactly the same thing. When I asked a friend about this, he explained, "He does this for several hours every day. He practices until he can do it without even thinking about it. In this way, he can focus his energy on his audience."

Physical humor also can be unintentional, as when someone trips on a rug and is slightly embarrassed, but not hurt. Our laughter comes from an empathetic connection with the victim. A woman walking into a men's public restroom can be physical humor if the woman isn't drawn to tears of embarrassment. It also can be a casually focused and intentional act, as when someone deliberately uses physical humor to "lighten up" a situation or simply to gain attention. The game of Charades is an example of physical humor used for entertainment. It offers an opportunity for an enlivened social interaction because the communication is light-hearted.

2. Rational Humor

A magician has been working on a cruise ship using the same act for many years. The audiences like him, and the people change often enough that he doesn't have to worry about finding new tricks. The Captain's parrot sits in the back row and watches the magician's act night after night, year after year. After a while, the parrot figures out how the tricks work and starts giving the secrets away to the audiences. When the magician makes a bouquet of flowers disappear, for instance, the parrot squawks, "Behind his back! Behind his back!" Well, the magician gets annoyed at this, but does nothing because the pesky bird belongs to the Captain. One day, the ship springs a leak and sinks. The magician manages to survive by grabbing a plank of wood and floating on it, while the parrot flies over and sits on the other end. They drift and drift for three days. On the morning of the fourth day, the parrot finally looks over at the magician and says, "Okay, I give up. Where did you hide the ship?"

This is a story styled form of humor often used in social situations to illustrate a point. The context of this story is the tension we feel when blocked from accomplishing a task. It is part of the world in which we live.

Many texts define rational humor as that which we deliberately and consciously induce, control and create. In other words, rational humor is humor that develops from the world that we know. For the same reason, rational humor is predictable and uses the symbols familiar to us. Most rational humor follows along in logical manner. Most humor and comedy is rational because it springs from commonly shared, life scenarios, things that "make sense."

Paradoxically, nonsense humor is actually another form of rational humor. For example, we might wonder how much deeper the ocean would be if it contained no sponges. Obviously, there is no relationship between sponges and ocean depth, but it has logic of its own. So, too, does the question, "If you could have everything, where would you put it?" Funny to children, they often get these nonsense jokes faster than the adults.

Children live in a world dominated by giants. Children also live in a world that to them does not make sense. They conform because they are powerless to do otherwise. Clowns use a lot of nonsense humor with children. A clown might say to a child, "Light travels faster than sound. That's why some people appear bright until they open their mouths and say something."Or, "What are your sister's five favorite words?" Answer: "I am going to tell!" You can see how "nonsense" really makes a lot of sense in a backhanded kind of way. Both children and the elderly respond readily to nonsense humor as they both live in a world that makes little sense to them.

Most humor comes to us from the rational world in which we live. Thus, most of the "tools" that empower us to use humor fall into this category. There are many and varied academic kinds of rational humor, I have compressed them into the following five: (1) Metaphors, (2) Puns and Riddles, (3) Exaggeration and Understatements, (4) Ambiguity and Incongruity and, (5) Satire and Deviation. Giving titles to these forms makes them specific as tools for understanding and using humor.

Metaphors

One tool is the ability to compare one thing to another in such a way as to drive home a point. The listener must make the connection. William says to Gillian one day, "Your dad seems to get along well with your pet Tyrannosaurus Rex. I guess that's because no one would want to argue with twelve tons of unstoppable fury." To which Gillian replies, "Hey, watch it! That's my dad you're talking about!"

Humor does not come out of nothing. Comparisons originate from our perceptions of reality, experience and feeling. In the above example, likening the power of a dinosaur to the power of a father, creates the humor. This comparison of like and unlike things is "metaphor." For example, the phrase a "storm of protest" unites images of intense weather with intense emotions. Although a literal storm and a literal outburst of objections have nothing whatsoever to do with each other, this metaphor brings a highly defined image to mind. "Nipped in the bud" combines images of pruning a garden with cutting off a new idea or project.

Metaphors can be amusing because at first they seem to be false or contradictory. Humor that is based on metaphorical structure uses contradictory comparisons at a literal level. An example might be a bumper sticker reading "Honk if you love peace and quiet." Silly, isn't it? The literal truth is that most people appreciate peace and quiet. The deviation or contradiction to this literal truth is that you're asked to make a loud obnoxious noise to indicate agreement. This type of humor often leads to an impossible absurdity, i.e., making a loud noise in support of silence and peacefulness. The typical reaction is usually laughter or pleasurable amusement at the blatant contradiction. Herein we see how rational, humorous metaphors often include absurdity or contradictions.

Puns and Riddles

Puns are humorous because they have double meanings, such as "Hello, I'm the doctor's nurse," and the response, "Really. I didn't know he was ill." Puns are fun because they are simple, and often the opportunity to create a pun develops quite naturally within our normal, everyday conversations. Because of this, puns are a great place to start flexing your humor muscles.

Puns and riddles are so common that you can use them in any topic of discussion. Around the office you might inject this riddle: Question: "What do you get when you put a kitten in a Xerox machine?" Answer: "A copycat." Another one I like is: "What do you get when you cross an elephant with a peanutbutter jar?" Answer: You get an elephant that sticks to the roof of your mouth and a peanutbutter jar with a long memory." Riddles are closely associated with puns because they often use words that have double meanings. "What's a Grecian urn?" The response: "Depends on his line of work" swaps the word "urn" with "earn." Riddles are a form of humor that most of us are introduced to at an early age because they are simple and easy to remember. *"What did the mayonnaise say to the refrigerator?" "Close the door, I'm dressing." "How do you keep a skunk from smelling?" "Hold its nose."* Sometimes the answers are elusive enough that persons joining in will give up and ask for the answer. Riddles are great games to play with youngsters, exaggeration allowing each participant to take a turn. Riddles are also a quick and easy way to change attitudes, stop an argument or simply make fun out of a boring situation.

Exaggeration and Understatement

While puns and riddles are usually simple occasions for laughter, exaggeration and understatements are forms of humor used to educate or make a point. In a conversation that focused on the overuse of credit, I inserted this exaggeration: "I asked a clerk, 'Do you honor credit cards' and he responded, 'We not only honor them, but we love and obey them.'" This demonstrated the extent that stores will go to attract your business. Then there is the exaggeration, "He's so dull, he couldn't entertain a doubt" — stretching the idea of a dull personality to the point of absurdity. In both cases, the speaker is trying to make a point in an entertaining fashion. "Dumb as a post" or "a few cards short of a deck" are common phrases that are exaggerations of our perceptions of another person. "He has a B.A., an M.A. and a PhD but no J.O.B." takes the position that the amount of education does not guarantee getting employed.

Understatement is the opposite of exaggeration and is a very effective tool to defuse uncomfortable situations or intense emotions. *Two people are in a car doing 70 MPH on a freeway. Directly ahead of them, a semi tractor-trailer suddenly careens, then rolls over on its side and slides along the pavement; sparks flying everywhere. The driver of the car is able to do nothing but slow down. The semi ahead bursts into flames and then separates from its trailer load, creating a small space between them. The car with the passengers manages to pass between the two halves of the semi, with only inches on each side. Now safely past the wreck, the driver of the car comes to a stop at the side of the road. Still holding the wheel in a white-knuckled grip, he takes a deep breath, turns to his passenger and says flatly, "That was close."* Understatement is a dry sort of humor used to defuse the intensity of a given situation or reality.

Ambiguity and Incongruity

Ambiguity and incongruity are examples of humor that inadvertently appear in our environment. You are at the airport where you see a sign that reads, "We take your bags and send them in all directions." Makes you stop for a minute, doesn't it? In a newspaper you read, "Their request for weapons was not greeted with open arms." On a roadway in Chicago there is a sign saying "Chicago. The city that works," but the sign is upside down. A job applicant, describing the strengths of his personality, says, "Humility is the best part of my personality." These are all examples of the inadvertent humor that is all around us. To find such humor is to find a treasure of joy and the realization that we are all humans who makes mistakes.

Satire and Value Deviation

Satire and value deviation are subtle forms of humor that must be used carefully as they are forms that, when used recklessly, can offend or hurt others. Satire uses ridicule, sarcasm and irony to expose, attack or put-down some aspects of our lives.

Satire traditionally takes some part of reality and turns it into a "spoof" or pokes fun at the situation. Gilbert and Sullivan were masters at satire. Their operettas satirize the

● ●

social life of British society around the 19th century. For example, the "H.M.S. Pinafore" song "When I was a Lad" pokes fun at ambitions of the upper class. Reality was that in 19th Century England, the first-born son of a wealthy family inherited the estate. The second born son went into the military. The third born son went into the ministry. The Gilbert and Sullivan operetta satirizes the 19th century, established British gentry in their lyrics:

I grew so rich that I was sent, by the pocket borough into Parliament.

I always voted at my party's call, and I never thought of thinking for myself at all.

Now landsmen all, whoever you may be, if you want to rise to the top of the tree.

If your soul isn't fettered to an office stool, be careful to be guided by this golden rule.

Stick close to your desks, and never go to sea, and you may all be rulers of the Queen's Navy.

Obviously, this golden rule is the opposite of reality. Although dated by the social structures of the time, the contrast to what was the truth creates the humor. Extreme satire, however, may be considered by some to be rude and inappropriate.

Value deviation is humor that tries to challenge or shift what we consider important. Burping and other bodily function noises fall into this category. David is a twelve-year old boy who burps while eating. At school, his class-mates laugh when he burps. However, when he's with his family at home eating dinner a burp is cause for scolding.

While value deviation humor is anything but subtle, and can be pushed to the point of being harmful at worst and obnoxious at best, it always challenges our values. Much political, religious and sexual humor falls into this category. When the purpose of this humor is to change our attitudes, it can be effective. However, this type of humor may polarize listeners. If a listener agrees with the ridicule, it's experienced as humorous. However, if a listener has a serious bond with the subject, feelings of outrage or disdain can result.

Given its potentially volatile nature, satire and value deviation are forms of humor best used by professional comics or insightful therapists. Recently, humor in therapeutic settings has been acknowledged for its efficacy in defusing intense emotions long enough for the patient to be able to gain a different perspective. A counselor is working with a patient who threatens suicide to gain attention. The patient has never tried to commit suicide and exhibits a deep resentment towards the idea of death. The patient desires to extinguish this behavior. One day the patient is talking to his counselor and says, "I want to commit suicide!" The counselor responds, "Well, you know that this is your decision, but remember you have to live with it." This response might appear insensitive, but the patient quickly grasped the point of this satire and laughed. Satire can be a professional response to a patient who needs this kind of humor to help diffuse the intensity of an emotionally challenging situation. However, unless you're extremely confident of your audience and scenario, this kind of humor can end up placing your proverbial foot in your proverbial mouth! Use with caution!

Metaphors, riddles and puns, absurdity, exaggerations and understatements, ambiguity and incongruity, satire and value deviation are all forms of rational humor; created for a purpose and based on mutually understood and shared senses of "reality."

3. Irrational Humor

Irrational humor is a special category. Irrational humor starts with a rational concept and then disconnects taking you into a fantasy. Irrational humor subtly moves you from "reality" into nonsense (the exact opposite of how nonsense humor works). Irrational humor is a new concept with unlimited potential in the areas of counseling, therapy, product development and marketing.

In conversation, irrational humor might take you to the irrational by using a question. For example, a therapist is dealing with a child having social problems at school. The child is characterizing his teacher as a horrid individual. The child is becoming tense. The therapist might use a serious manner to ask, "So, how many heads does your teacher have?" The question throws the child out of balance for a moment. The use of an irrational question to separate the child from tension is different from nonsense humor. Nonsense humor makes sense from nonsense. Irrational humor makes nonsense out of sense. In therapeutic settings, irrational humor can be like "shock treatment" in that it briefly disconnects the mind and provides a window of opportunity for the therapist to enter and professionally alter the patient's attitude or perception. Irrational humor is also a way to establish rapport. The intensity of a shared irrational humor experience enables therapists to bridge distances with a patient through laughter and establishing a foundation of the acceptability of "mistakes," without judgments.

Much of therapy is designed to help the client think through a problem. The use of puppets is a common tool to help clients distance themselves from the emotions of their situation. Irrational humor can be used for the same purpose. Sally was a delightful, freckled-faced 12-year old child in a special education class. Sally had a compulsive fixation about shoes. She liked or disliked a person based on the kinds of shoes he or she wore. One day, Sally angrily tried to take the shoes off another child's feet. Her teacher took her aside and asked her about the problem. After Sally explained her anger, her teacher asked, "So, what did the shoes say about how you feel?" in order to pull Sally out of her fixation. "What are you talking about?" asked Sally, "I want to rip those shoes off her!" The teacher responded, "Well, I was just wondering how the shoes would feel about all of this." Offering an irrational perspective in this humorous, light-hearted way interrupted Sally's obsession long enough for her teacher to be able to guide her out of anger.

Irrational humor is not a panacea for dealing with people and their problems. The overuse or misuse of irrational humor can run the risk of appearing as ridicule. It takes perception and experience to know when you are starting to cross the line from humor to putting a person down or insulting their intelligence. But, the selective power of irrational humor to entertain or enlighten is unmistakable.

Clowns symbolize irrational humor. Their very existence takes you into a fantasy land of humor and comedy. The costume of a professionally dressed clown is a prime example of irrational humor. The costume itself conforms to all the proper characteristics of normal clothing. The costumes are neat and clean, the design is clear and distinctive and the accessories add to the general appearance of the costume. However, a clown's costume is full of "mistakes." The clown wears shoes, but the shoes are too big! A tie might be present, but it's too small. Buttons loom, collars tower. All the elements of clothing are present, but the costume itself irrationally contradicts what we consider normal dress. We see it, but the proportions do not make sense. Clown makeup is similarly fashioned along the fastidiously strict guidelines of applying makeup, but extends the design and color beyond the bounds of rational thought. It is that extreme originality that creates the humor.

Irrational humor is an important form of humor because it "disarms" us. Irrational humor suspends you in a mistake, but you accept the mistake as a "good" mistake that will not harm. Clowns extend the experience of the irrational from face and costume into conversation. For example, a clown says to a child, "What is your name?" The child replies, "My name is Mary." The clown continues, "My, what a beautiful name, Mary. How long have you been Mary — Mary?" The child looks blank. Her mind is trying to connect the rational concept of her name within a time framework. If this connection does not take place, the child looks up to her mother and says, "Mommy?" At that point, the clown might follow up with the escape: "How old are you?" This allows the child to connect back to the rational and respond with her correct age. Good humor always makes fun of yourself and not the listener. Good clowns never squirt water or other material onto the audience. Clowns terminate their relationships with their client on a friendly and positive relationship.

This is the Twenty First Century. The time has come to take humor and comedy seriously. The power of humor can greatly improve the quality or life. Humor enables you to make friends and can distance you from unpleasant situations. Humor is a highly useful tool for exploring and questioning our society, institutions, language, meanings, concepts and our own actions and beliefs. It can heal, comfort and entertain.

Many books have been written on all the various categories, subcategories and types of humor, but for our purposes, classifying humor and comedy into the three classifications of Physical, Rational and Irrational are sufficient to empower you to bring about those changes in your life and the lives of those near and dear to you. You can do this by understanding how each type of humor works.

Regardless of the category, most humor is still a "language game." Through voice inflection, facial expressions body language and a humorous perception of things, it's easy to live in a world of joy in which all your energy is directed to celebrate life and all it holds dear. All of us can create good humor once we are armed with clear and accurate understandings of what humor is and how it works. In the next chapter, we'll look at ways you can strengthen your own sense of humor as well as some ways you can share your humor with others.

Forrest "Muggins" Wheeler uses humor to knock down barriers of animosity in an ultra-conservative Muslim hospital in Kabul, Afghanistan.

Chapter Two

Putting the Power to Use

"How do you know you have power
unless you use it?"

Chapter 2 focuses on the ways you can use humor and comedy to:

1. Distance yourself from unpleasant situations.

2. Create friendships.

3. Use humor to create energy, enthusiasm and positive attitudes

Chapter Two

Putting the Power to Use

Through humor, you can soften some of the blows that life delivers.
And once you find laughter,
no matter how painful your situation might be,
you can survive it.

– Bill Cosby

Charlie was one of those ultra conservative, stiff-upper-lip, humorless individuals who disciplined his classroom with a single silent stare that could turn the most mischievous child's blood cold. That is, until the faculty Christmas party. For Charlie, a little alcohol went a long way. His voice became louder. The air filled with his ultra dry and often witless jokes. I heard one faculty member say; "When will Charlie grow up?" Her friend raised the question; "What is the difference between government bonds and men?" "I don't know," was the reply, "What is the difference between government bonds and men?" "Bonds mature!" was the knowledgeable answer.

Humor often conflicts with our ideas of mature behavior. Although comedians such as Red Skelton and

Danny Kaye are historically persons of outstanding skill, too often we view humor as little more than silly. When I retired from a long career as a school administrator, I felt isolated, living in a world in which I no longer belonged or had a useful function. A friend invited me to volunteer with him as a clown in a local hospital.

Keep in mind; my background was firmly rooted in the serious and sober world of academia. The idea of dressing up as a clown of all things, struck me as blatantly ridiculous. However, out of sheer boredom, I accepted his invitation to observe competition at a Pacific Shrine Clown convention. There, I discovered the power of clowns to use play activities to teach children. Best of all, these clowns were having fun. To my astonishment, the children attending the convention played openly with the clowns and responded to their encouragement without reservation. Something magical was happening and I wanted in on the action. After six months of supervision and training in costume, face and humor, I became a "caring clown."

Volunteering as a clown, providing joy and happiness to those children, helped me overcome the depression I experienced at retirement. Their laugh became my laugh. Their fresh new appreciation renewed my energy for things I had long forgotten. Through this involvement, my own sense of humor has strengthened and expanded. Over the years, the benefits of giving joy, comfort and humor through clowning have overflowed into all areas of my life. I have developed a wide new community of friends in several countries and have realized a sense of usefulness that will last the rest of my days.

These new friendships have brought me right into the middle of the electronic world. Have you noticed that we live in a world of electronic messaging? I telephone to communicate some information and find myself bombarded with electronic information that I do not want to know. Personal computers, newspapers, television and mass media, constantly bombard us with messages of fear, terrorism and incompetence. Messages like the imminence of war or that our children are vulnerable to predators. Many of my friends find themselves shielding themselves from other human beings and from what they see as an unpredictable, chaotic environment. They feel potentially victimized by a never-ending variety of new, dangerous viruses. They can't leave home for fear of assault. They are continuously informed that our businessmen, politicians and authority figures are untrustworthy.

True or not, do these messages condition us to feel fearful? Is this consistent and persuasive message of fear eroding our confidence in ourselves as well as our ability to trust others? I feel sorry for the elderly, the uneducated and those already suffering from depression, who are vulnerable to a constant stream of one-sided negative information.

All of this media hype helps to create a stressful world in which to live. You rise in the morning to hear the news tell you are about to be attacked by terrorists, your favorite teacher of household hints is an accused felon, pedophiles are about to molest your children, there are "worms" and viruses attacking your computer, and the stock market just wiped out your painfully accumulated investments. If that were not bad enough, the freeway is a lineal parking lot and your work load requires 28 hours of labor to be condensed into 6 hours of time.

Stress and tension are part of everyday life. Relief and comfort may come from routines that make us comfortable. We brush our teeth the same way each day; we drive along familiar routine routes. Routine tells us all is right with the world. We also seek relief and comfort through isolation. We use television, videotapes and computers to entertain us in the comfort and safety of our own homes. Humor enables us to modify or delete media that creates stress and replace it with media experiences that reduce stress.

But is self-isolation our only option? Perhaps humor offers us a better alternative. When we access humor we cope with a world obsessed with images of fear and danger. Laughter allows us to step away from the bondage of media hype. We make fun of what we cannot change, allowing us to focus our energy on those things that are within our range of control. Isolation and fear often results in increased body fat. Humor enables us to take the guilt out of being fat. Humor combines with diet and exercise to maintain weight control.

Negativity and isolation are expectable outcomes when we live and work in impersonal, sterile environments surrounded by multitudes of people we never get to know. Humor helps us become aware of what we are feeling and enables us to choose alternative ways to see the world in which we live. Humor helps us make the shift from anger or fear to laughter.

It is the end of the day and you are very tired. As you enter the bus to go home, you see two empty seats. One seat is beside a person who looks quiet, perhaps a little depressed. The other seat is next to a person who is smiling, and seems to have had a great day. You might well choose the person who appears negative because he is not likely to talk to you. Why? Media hype or our work environment often leads to suppressed anger which conditions us to reject contact with others. When we feel stress, we do not feel like connecting, much less laughing or finding humor — particularly if the other person feels like playing.

This has not always been true. There was a time when it was common to hear people whistle, children playing "kick-the-can" in the streets, even families using residential street corners to play baseball. Fifty years ago, neighbors would say "hello" and greet others with a friendly smile and a "tip of the hat." As a family, we ate together, played together and stayed together. Have we lost our sense of community and connection? Have we lost our sense of humor? Perhaps the time has come to take humor seriously!

Denying Our Sense of Humor

From early childhood, you and I were taught that seriousness is a mark of intelligence and maturity. Schools teach us that education must take place in a serious environment. Hospitals are environments laced with the serious issues of health and healing. Doctors, nurses and health practitioners see using humor as a compromise to the integrity of their positions. "After all," said one doctor, "humor might destroy my professional integrity." Likewise, religious institutions teach us that getting to know God is serious business: ministers of the faith must portray a somber and serious profile. We've actually been taught and conditioned to feel threatened by humor.

While it's socially acceptable to passively enjoy humor in a performance, being humorous in most areas of life is often viewed as a mark of the inept or immature. In order to be heard, we must be serious. For younger generations, the desire may be seen as "cool," sometimes projected as arrogance and aloofness. We've been conditioned to become so overly focused on being serious that we actively suppress our sense of humor. In this technological and personally isolated world, there seems to be no room for the humor that will make our very existence more bearable, enjoyable and effective.

Humor Helps with Anger

When you can choose between humor and anger, why choose anger? Anger is unnecessary, counterproductive and generates ever-increasing anger, eventually escalating to emotions of rage. Yet, humor is an easily accessible tool for defusing our emotions of anger, stress and frustration. *A man was eating fish and chips at a sidewalk café. A woman walked by with a small dog. The dog growled and started barking at the man's food. "Can I throw him a bit?" asked the man. "Of course," said the lady. So the man picked up the dog and threw it over a nearby wall.* You might not want to share this story with someone who loves dogs, but you cannot be condemned for privately enjoying this kind of humor. Give yourself permission for humor to become part of your life, because it does not work if one is too serious. Accept humor as a secret weapon against anger.

"Waiter, there's a fly in my soup!" The waiter responds, "Not fussy about what they eat, are they?"

We can train ourselves to find humor in the frustrations or mistakes of daily life. We can think of a humorous situation when feeling angry. We can replace the thought that is producing anger with a thought that produces humor. (It gets easier with practice.) Even simple jokes can help:

"Waiter, how often do you change the tablecloths?" "I don't know sir; I've only been here six months."

We can use humor to deflect anger addressed against you. Humor can also be used to acknowledge someone else's anger: *"My spouse has an even disposition — always mad."*

I often use toys to deal with stress. My favorite is a "Groucho Marx Mask." When stalled in traffic, I put it on and wave at the people beside me. They usually (but not always) smile back. (Have you ever noticed that when driving, those who drive slower are retarded and those who drive faster are maniacs?) I purchase humorous audio tapes and music, because playing them while driving allows me a place of refuge from the stress of urban congestion.

Something that used to irritate me was people who got in the express lane of a store with more than the allowed number of items. I used to glower at them, until once it ended up in a major confrontation. So, I purchased some 3-D monster glasses at a magic store, which I put on. When I peered into their basket and started counting the items, they get the idea, but the humor keeps them from confrontation.

• •

As you expose yourself to the humor around you, there comes a time when you want to share this experience more and more with others. Sharing a humorous experience is sharing your understanding of the mistakes around you, as well as expressing your personal feelings and interpretations. A friend of mine once told me about standing in line at the post office. This particular station was small and always congested, taking an inordinate amount of time to achieve simple mailing tasks. Feeling her irritation mount, she made a remark to another person in line about how long it always seemed to take to get things done at that particular post office.

A man behind them said, "I came in the other day and there was no one here; I was in and out in five minutes."

"Really?" she responded, "What magical hour of the day does this takes place?"

According to my friend, the other people in line all chuckled and there was a noticeable easing of tension. At the same time, the postal workers, overhearing this, speeded up their efforts and the line moved much faster.

Using humor in this manner allowed her to voice her frustration, experience a casual bonding through shared sympathies with the strangers around her and exert a positive change in how long it took to complete her business at the post office. Not bad for a one-liner, and much preferable to stewing silently in frustration.

In addition to short-circuiting feelings of anger, sharing humorous incidents or observations with others is the easiest way of moving from passivity toward becoming a humorous person. Here is a mistake I found humorous: *I once interviewed a woman who claimed to be forty. She said she had no proof of her date of birth, however, because the birth record had been at a city hall that burned down (sixty years ago).*

As you become humorous, you become a more pleasant and delightful person whom other people will want to know. Becoming humorous allows you to take charge of your life because it grants you the ability to look at a situation from at least two points of view and to choose how you want to experience something. Developing a sense of humor also helps you connect with people around you, and develop supportive and encouraging relationships. In this way, humor also helps lift feelings of loneliness. reducing depression and building self esteem.

Humor as a Healing Force

Is it true that your body can't maintain tension and laugh at the same time? Imagine that two people are carrying a couch. One starts to laugh. That person cannot both carry his end of the couch and laugh; they must set it down. Why? *Because laughter makes the muscles relax.*

We are now in the Twenty First Century. The Association of Applied and Therapeutic Humor has evidence that humor reduces stress, boosts immunity, relieves pain, decreases anxiety, stabilizes mood, enhances communication, inspires creativity and bolsters morale which we discussed in Chapter 1. These things all reduce tension, which is why humor is such a vital and effective tool for surviving in today's fear-driven world. Humor is a vastly underutilized resource, and yet, it's all around us. All we have to do is be willing to recognize and utilize the humor that already exists. And the best news is that a good sense of humor is a skill anyone can develop.

Flexing Your Humorous Muscles

You develop skills with humor by practicing humor more and more every day. When you think and apply humor you strengthen the skills to apply humor to different situations. Skill development from humor can help you achieve the following goals:

- Be Sociable. *Two men were talking. One says proudly to the other, "I have six boys." The other guy says, "That's a nice sized family. I wish I had six children." The proud father of six boys says with a note of sympathy, "Don't you have any children?" The first man replied, "Yeah, ten!"*

- Seem Clever. An obstreperous child is trying to give you a "bad" time. So you ask, "Tell me. *What is a characteristic specimen of metamorphism possessing a parallel stratification?"* You just pulled the plug on his antics as he tries to figure out what you said.

- Make a Critical Point. You may not think humor could work well in this area, but often, humor helps us share profound truths upon which we can all agree. *"We should be glad that God does not give us everything we ask for."*

- Enjoy the little things in life, such as pleasant feelings we get at the giggle of a small child, the joy of a beautiful sunset or the sense of sharing from story-telling. Life always feels better when you lighten things up.

- Express something one could not otherwise express. Humor is very effective for expressing ideas that might otherwise be hard for someone else to receive or hear; it softens criticism. Using humor to deliver a critique allows the listener to feel you have a problem with their "behavior," but is not rejecting them as a person. Students often receive papers submitted to their teachers covered with negative comments and red marks. The very sight of this treasured document, so mutilated, makes your blood run cold. If the instructor would put a smiling face with the comment, "I can help you with this. See me at our break." Applied this way, humor allows us to practice the principle that being *kind* is more important than simply being *right*.

We can understand how we use humorous jokes to empower ourselves when we ask the following questions: Why am I telling the joke? Am I trying to impress? Do I want to distance myself from this person? Is there something I am trying to inform? If you are listening to humor, what is the person trying to do? When you learn a joke ask yourself what does the joke really say or express? Humor is more than telling jokes.

Humor allows us to experience the aesthetic pleasure of an absurd situation. *"My wife has two hobbies. She swims and she knits. It makes the wool a little soggy, but if she is happy then I am happy."*

Humor in general, and jokes specifically, can be used as a way of rebelling. It is a way of renouncing allegiance or subjugation. We may revolt against oppressive parents, society, values, prohibitions, church rules, faulty theories and friends, etc. Adolescents may especially have desires to escape from restrictions set by parents and teachers. Specialists use the term "value deviation humor" when using humor to escape from the norms of society. I often hear my grandson say "Duhh", "Soo" or "Hello?" to announce a challenge to some family tradition or expected behavior. With humor, we are able to acceptably say "unacceptable" things. The overstatement: "Come on, give this little kid a chance." is more acceptable than saying; "You cannot make me!" You can relieve frustration with jokes about mother-in-law, the boss, teacher, sex, alcohol and one's spouse. Children often find humor in taboo bathroom topics, breaking rules and censored information. There are many forms of humor and many ways to apply it.

Developing Humor

If you find yourself in an isolated world, set apart, without care or concern for those with whom you come into contact, perhaps it is time to let the healing power of humor into your life starting with awareness of the humor around you. You may not be able to control others, but you can control yourself through humor. Humor allows us to shift our point of view. It allows us to see things from a different perspective. Observing humor, and playfully applying it in our daily lives, empowers us to feel connected to the rest of humanity. As I mentioned earlier, the line between anger and laughter is razor thin. Because of this, laughter can evict feelings of anger and frustration simply by observing and acknowledging the many humorous situations that arise all around you. *Empowerment through humor is so simple that it starts by just being willing to see it.*

Let's say you're going to start a new business. You hire a caterer to set up the food and decorations for your opening day ceremonies. The day of the ceremony, you arrive and expect to find a ribbon you ordered across the buffet table. Oops, the ribbon is in place, but it says "Rest in Peace." Your first reaction is to be angry. Instead, you recall the words printed on the ribbon you really ordered and envision a funeral home where a ribbon hangs, reading "Good Luck at Your New Location." Now just try to feel angry! The ability to choose, to shift your perspective, is always yours. Humor empowers you to be independent of, and to enjoy more control of, any given situation.

Finding humor in the frustrations of daily life is easy. Simply change your focus from looking for the pain — to looking for the "fun." *Humor is really nothing more than an emotion and emotions can be harnessed and improve*d. So, make a conscious choice to find the humor everywhere you go. Once, I found myself trapped on a slow moving freeway when the thought occurred to me that it took my great grandfather four months to cross the country in a covered wagon. At the rate I was traveling, I thought my great grandfather had made rather good time.

Every time you laugh, your body is telling you that you're experiencing a new or different perspective. For example, the other day, I found a new perspective on my own aging when I discovered how tired I was because my street had become so long. This observation helps me deal with the reality of aging. Maybe I can't choose the way aging affects me physically, but I *can* choose how I *feel* about it.

We need a sense of humor to deal with the chaos and irrational nature of life. We were raised believing that if we did the right thing, had a good education, our lives would be smooth. This is not the reality most of us encounter. Our society is uncertain and unpredictable. We don't like to admit that we're less than perfect and we don't like feeling insecure. Of course, the real price of taking ourselves too seriously is that we start to believe that life is serious and heavy; we get puffed up with self-importance. When we take life seriously and allow ourselves to feel self-important, we put ourselves into the position of being hurt. It's not a very effective way to go through the ups and downs of life and it certainly limits the amount of enjoyment a person is able to experience.

A doctor went up to his patient in a home for the aged. His patient did not recall who he was, even though he had been his doctor for several years. So the doctor said, "Ben, don't you know who I am?" "No" he replied, "but if you go to the front desk a nurse can help you." The doctor had one perspective of concern for his patient. The patient another perception of concern for his doctor's loss of memory.

The ability to see the incongruity and ambiguity allows us to see the humor of the situation. And when we see humor, we can harness it as a natural, spontaneous quality in everyday life that empowers us and helps us manage stress.

It is simple and easy to develop a sense of humor by exposing yourself to humor, Check out humorous videos and books or watch comedy on TV. In addition, actively looking for humor helps you develop a sense of humor. I like to watch people in public places like the airport and shopping malls. At the airport, I watched a family buying fried chicken to eat on the plane. The picture I created in my mind of the smell of fresh, fried chicken, wafting over the heads of all the other passengers with their little packages of roasted peanuts, amused me. It was just a little thought, but it made me smile. Speaking of airports, have you ever wondered how airport security can spot the tiniest nail file, but still manage to lose your luggage? It may seem a little macabre, but I like to watch people trying to manage several pieces of luggage plus their children. (Perhaps it's not as entertaining to them as it is to me.) People in stores are fun to watch. The other day I watched a new competitive sport: a child was throwing items out of the shopping cart just as fast as the mother was putting them in. Once, when a clerk at the checkout register asked me if I had found everything I was looking for, I said I wasn't sure, then asked if there was anything else hidden in the back.

The more you expose yourself to the humor around you the more you become aware of humor. Eventually, your total attitude towards life begins to change as you subliminally digest the diverse and pervasive humor in your world.

Here is an exercise you will want to try:

List all the things that stress you out. Look at your list. It may contain such things as financial problems, personal relationships, declining health and problems on the job. These are all things over which you have little or no control. Thinking about them creates unpleasant feelings.

Now make a list of all the things that have happened to you that gave you pleasure (be specific). Do you feel more "light hearted" when your memory shifts you from a more stressful perspective to a joyful one?

You cannot change the world you live in, but you can change your point of view. Just by thinking of the things that make you happy, you can make yourself happy. When you feel depressed, try recalling humorous or pleasant memories from the past, and see if it shifts your mood. If you have memorabilia of pleasant experiences, bring them out and look them over. Mementos and treasures of this kind can "trigger" happy thoughts and feelings. This is another way of accessing humor.

Practice Making 'Imperfect' Perfect

The first person you begin to practice your humor skills on is perhaps the last person you would think of as being a good choice. That person is you! Why not? Throughout your life, you've used yourself as a third person for venting your feelings. Talking to yourself to express anger, frustration or to practice an anticipated conversation is an everyday experience for most of us. So, why not use yourself to practice humor?

1. Start practicing humor when you are alone. In the privacy of your home, practice laughing aloud. You might start with something both easy and simple. Starting with a short and perhaps soft laugh, progressively laugh louder and harder. The next time you have the opportunity; sustain your laugh for longer and longer periods. This may seem like a simple technique but believe me it really works!

2. Another thing you can do is make silly faces at yourself in the mirror. Developing facial expres-

sions and laughing patterns in the mirror shows you how you appear to others Knowing how we look to others is important because we often project impressions unknowingly. With this exercise, you gain greater skill in what you convey to others with your expressions. By using exaggerated faces, you train the facial muscles to reflect emotional moods. You might try silly, serious, mad, loving and nonsensical facial expressions. The activities of laughing and practicing exaggerated faces combine together to energize your expressions and increase your laughter "vocabulary."

3.   Now that you're comfortable and familiar with your own laughter and facial expressions, you might like to practice sharing humor with others. In order to develop and hone your skills and comfort levels with humor, you may want to start with puns and riddles. Puns consist of taking similar words and using them in a different meaning. Some examples of puns:

"Only three people showed up so we cannot have a forum."
"I quit teaching math when my parrot Polygon died."

Riddles are problems or a puzzle in the form of a question. For example:

"How can I find a cat?" Answer: "Look in a catalogue."
"Should a woman have children after forty?" Answer: "No, forty is enough."

There are nearly endless supplies and collections of "Knock Knock" jokes. For example:

"Knock, knock." "Who's there?" Answer: "Sigrid."
"Sigrid who?" Answer: "Sigrid Service."

Sometimes your audience will react with a "Yuk!" Remember, a "yuk" is as good as a laugh. Try some of these out on your friends who have young children. You will enlarge your repertoire of puns and riddles as children try their nonsense humor on you.

How Humor Helps

You can apply humor in a variety of situations. You can use it to help people by:

1. **Being persuasive.** My friend George was very adamant about who he wanted as our next governor. He became angry when I was not coming around to his point of view. I cannot change George, but I can decide how to deal with the situation. I could become defensive and combative, or I could employ humor. I chose to tell George that his choice repre- sented a real politician. A real politician can say absolutely nothing and mean it. His choice was also a good politician because he looks ahead and plans his mistakes carefully. Isn't it a shame that all the people who know how to run the country are driving cabs? George changed the subject. I used humor to create a window of opportunity for George to recon- sider his position without loss of pride or integrity. Creating neutrality is the first step in being persua- sive.

2. **Reduce defensiveness.** All a person needs is a hand to hold and a humorous heart to understand. Utilizing humor can let the other person know that

you're on the same side and that there's nothing to be defensive about, or that it's okay to have differing viewpoints.

3. **Change negative emotions into positive ones.** *"I had a horrible accident, but the doctor said he would soon have me walking. He was correct; I had to sell my car to pay his bill."* It's easy to have obsessive thoughts about a negative situation. By consciously choosing to turn your mind to humorous thoughts, the loop of negative thoughts can be broken and your mood will lighten.

4. **Ease tension.** Many situations in life arise, which are socially awkward or tense. Introducing humor can create the levity and the space for everyone to stop, breathe and relax. It's probably why people appreciate a funny person. *Two guys started to argue about politics. Finally a third guy said; "O.K. you guys, if you can't be kind, at least be vague."*

5. **Get attention.** People often say that one quality they look for in a mate or partner is humor, because people with humor are more enjoyable. Learning to find and harness humor in life's flow of conversation and events can make you more attractive to others and can leave a positive, lasting impression.

6. **Help another become accepted.** Criticism is a difficult thing to deliver to anyone, especially someone to whom you are close. Utilizing humor can defuse the delicacy of the situation and help another person overcome initial defensiveness. Using humor in this manner can help another person hear and apply your input. Mary was always giving unsolicited and unwanted advice at card games. One day, after several long sessions of advice that was

obviously unwanted, her friend said; *"You know Mary, advice can be a very good thing to pass on, because you won't use it anyway."*

When you become aware of the role of humor and practice the incorporation of humor in day-to-day conversations, you unconsciously start calling upon the power of humor to cope with problems and frustrations. Whether driving down the highway or in a conversation you find yourself very confident and in control. When you develop the characteristics of humor you access reason more clearly. This sense of clarity and objectivity enables you to work more successfully with others by reducing arguments and games of dominance. For example, when dealing with that person who criticizes weathermen in order to dominate a conversation your response could be, *"All of us could take a lesson from the weather. It also pays no attention to criticism."* Using humor to associate differences with mistakes rather than differences between individuals continues the empowerment of humor. *"The other night I ate at a real family restaurant. Every table had an argument going."* Humor allows us to overcome the impossible and elevate ourselves above it.

Protective Aspects of Humor

Sometimes we find ourselves in sticky situations in which we feel judged. There isn't much we can do about the attitudes that others adopt against us. However, coping with such difficulties is much easier when we use humor. Defensive humor may include "unconscious" or illogical ways of speaking. Defensive humor is a spontaneous reaction, when thrust unexpectedly into an uncomfortable situation. One example might be when smokers find themselves rudely confronted by non-smokers. A possible response using humor as a defense would be something like, *"Sure I smoke, but I eat only organically grown vegetables."*

A person may crack a joke to distract or change the conversation. You're not a wealthy person but find yourself surrounded by those who are, and they all seem to fixate the conversation on money. A way to use humorous tactics to change the topic of conversation would be, *"I started out with nothing, and I still have most of it."*

Humor can also displace or take something out of its normal context. The statements, *"It's hard to make a comeback when you haven't been anywhere,"* or *"The situation is hopeless, but not serious,"* are examples of displacement. You can defend yourself through depersonalizing. If asked, *"Why did you go to college, anyway?"* You might say, *"I didn't have anything else to do."* Or you can move the conversation to outright escape from reality. *"These days, I spend a lot of time thinking about the hereafter. I go somewhere to get something and then wonder what I'm here after."*

Humor in the Workplace

The workplace requires a high degree of competence in specific skills. Did you know, however, that the desire for perfection increases stress and tension, actually reducing a person's ability to find solutions? People strive so hard to do exactly what they feel is expected of them, they become blinded to creative solutions.

The workplace creates a façade of harmony where harmony normally would not exist. We work with people with whom we normally would not associate. We are sometimes asked to practice procedures that contradict our faith, our personal feelings or our sense of right and wrong. We cannot change the work environment, but we can use humor to change our perception of our working conditions. Using humor in the workplace is a powerful tool for (1) acknowledging that a problem exists, (2) stimulating and changing perspectives and creative processes to deal with the problem, and (3) finding new solutions by seeing the problem from a new perspective. We will deal in depth with this issue in chapter five on gender.

From an administrative point of view, humor is supportive, potent and facilitative. Humor can help employees to brainstorm ideas. Using humor gets and keeps attention in memos. Humor enhances motivation by reducing risks and stress. The use of humor provides a pleasurable and nurturing work experience. Employees can generate a more creative, productive effort when it is used for easing tension. People are simply more productive when they're relaxed and as I stated earlier, laughter will make the body relax. It should not be surprising that positive humor generates greater productivity in the workplace than does negative humor such as satire, "put-down" humor or mockery.

Supervisors are in a unique position to incorporate humor and laughter into work relationships. Types of humor the supervisor might use include (a) over-and-understate-ments, (b) incongruity, (c) unexpectedness or surprise, (d) revelation of truth and, (e) word plays. Though negative humor is generally unproductive, positive humor seems to be a useful managerial tool for both genders. Managers may find employees quite receptive to humor and, when humor is practiced with discernment, they can increase their administrative effectiveness by using it to improve commu-nications with subordinates. Naturally, discretion and appropriateness are part of this mix. Using humor to avoid serious topics is inappropriate. Conversely, sexist, racist and put-down humor should be avoided at all costs. For the best results, humor should take place with an attitude of "play."

Humor is a quality associated with successful leaders and managers. In his 1998 article "Want to be a Successful Manager?" G. Barbour writes: "Humor's potential as a managerial tool is facilitated by identifying the four functions of humor: 1) facilitates learning, 2) helps change behavior, 3) promotes increased creativity and 4) helps us feel less threatened by change."

On one occasion while attending a conference at a Holiday Inn in Toronto, Ontario Canada, I discovered an unusual example of humor fully utilized in the workplace. It is at Holiday Inn on King Street. This convention styled hotel is full-blown clown. That's right. From Hotel Manager, Marlin Kaeranen to the waiter that serves the customers, all are clowns. Not only is clowning at this hotel accepted, it is expected and incorporated into their training program. They do not dress in clown face and costume when at work, but volunteer as clowns in and around the community. While the executive staff found that having a staff of clowns was good marketing, they also discovered the beneficial side effects of easier management because the resultant humor from clowning created a common bond between management and staff. The employee skills developed in learning to become a clown transferred into strengths for employees dealing with the public. In addition, the clown training reduced turnover in staff, created higher employee efficiency and lowered operating costs.

Slowly and with considerable resistance the world of work is beginning to see humor as a vehicle to improve productivity, stability and profit. As our society adapts to electronic and scientific choices, people will tend to mix and match work, recreation and type of preferred humor, into somewhat predictable lifestyles. These might include:

1. **Primarily Professional:** These people dedicate their life to a cause such as medicine, law, teaching or a corporate objective. They tend not to want a family nor do they want to marry. They are usually

highly trained and intelligent people who see their professional careers as both their life and recreation. These people tend to be urban and mobile and tend to see humor only as a vehicle to convince, persuade or influence. Their humor tends to be more oriented to their profession. It often reflects the frustration that can occur through the pressures of this kind of standard of living.

2. **Professionally Orientated:** These people are highly motivated towards a profession. They are more apt to change employers, and to seek other satisfaction outside of their profession. They have hobbies and recreational interests not related to their chosen field. They do not want children or a family. They are proud of their independence. Their personal relationships are many and varied. They seek out persons whose philosophy of life is similar to theirs. These people tend use humor to influence, but also to stimulate and entertain.

3. **Co-Partnership:** These people seek marriage and family. They see work, recreation and family as a matching of strengths against weaknesses. Both partners are working. They tend to live in suburban settings. They are competitive, setting high standards and expectations. The accumulation of "things" overshadows the accumulation of wealth. Humor is a source of entertainment, used to build cohesiveness and serves as a social lubricant.

4. **Traditional:** These people seek a traditional marriage where the man provides and the woman nurtures. They place family relationships ahead of material gain. They seek social and religious organizations that support traditional family values. They like to live in one community for a long time. They

tend to be conservative in politics and finance. Humor is for recreation and entertainment, and used to build cohesiveness in social groups.

5. **The Working Girl:** This reverse role scenario contrasts to the "Traditional." Here, the woman is the provider and serves either as a single mom or is married. If married, the male may take on the role of nurturer. This family unit tends to have few, but very close, friends. They are under pressure to change to a more traditional style family. Thus, they often live in a more rural community and stay very much to themselves. Humor serves to entertain, stimulate and influence.

6. **Recreational:** These people focus on recreation. Their work and social relationships are in support of recreation. They seldom marry. They avoid commitment and responsibility. They are very mobile and tend to rent in urban settings. They see humor as entertainment and as a social lubricant.

Humor and Mental Health

When we look back over the past twenty years, we realize that science and technology have outpaced our ability to adapt. The proliferation of displaced persons seen beneath bridges, dilapidated neighborhoods and public parks are but a small testimonial to our inability to meet the continued demands on our society. On the other hand, there have been broad and courageous advances in expanding the application of humor to medical and physical health. Institutions often have available humorous videos, old comedy radio programs and up-beat music. This material provides patients with the humor they need as an important part of their recovery. There have been significant advances in understanding humors' useful applications in therapy with the terminally ill. The use of clowns and puppets to facilitate communication between patient and therapist is increasing.

Humor is a good tool for dealing with anger and despondency. Humor is a vehicle to master self-confrontation. Just as having more compassion for ourselves allows us to extend more compassion to others, by seeing the humor of our own failings, we accept more readily the failings around us. Effective self-confrontation is not about self-blame, self-judging or self-punishment. Healthy self-confrontation is the ability to make an honest yet non-condemning assessment of one's life, decisions, actions and relationships. Humor also enables us to deal with past events, which can't be changed. Utilizing the power of humor can help our emotional and mental attitudes and strengthen many life-coping skills, including the ones listed below.

1. **Recognize that no one has a franchise on the truth.** There are as many viewpoints on reality as there are people. When our truth conflicts with someone else's, we can use humor to turn feelings of distress into a smile. Remember, truth is elusive when in love, drunk or running for office and while truth is often stranger than fiction, it isn't nearly as popular.

2. **Respect relational boundaries.** Our relationships with others have limitations based upon tradition and culture. Humor is a way of making fun of these irritations we have to live with. For example: *"I think of my 'in-laws' as pearls. They are always hanging around my neck. Actually, I solved the problem of relatives invading our home. I borrowed money from the rich ones and loaned it to the poor ones. Now none of them are around."*

3.   **Build practical solutions.** The practical solution places "cause and effect" as a substitute for emotional reactions, such as retaliation. The practical reality is that you only hurt yourself by seeking revenge. A Chinese proverb states, "Before retaliating, first dig two graves." Humor enables us to gain distance and see both sides of an issue or problem. Distancing ourselves from a problem enables us to see alternatives that help avoid stress and tension.

4.   **See the "Big Picture."** It is sometimes easy to be caught-up in the little irritations that plague us. Using humor, we can help ourselves put little things into their proper perspective. For example; I get irritated about electronic answering messages. The one that says how really important is my call, and how regretful it is that he is temporarily away from his desk. Just leave a message and he will immediately get back to me. My perception is that he is using his answering machine to screen his incoming calls. I like to leave an answer that gets my concern across. For example; "I'm terribly sorry that you are away from your desk because your competitor chooses to have a human talk directly to their customers." Like the old cliché, "Don't get mad — get even." By rising above our problems, we can see in new directions.

5.   **Shed the shame.** Let's face it; life has its embarrassing moments. *A group of conservative, elderly women was sitting around playing competitive snobbery. One woman says to the other, "I understand your daughter is looking for a job." "Why yes," came the reply, "My daughter is looking for something more challenging." At that point the*

daughter interjected, "That's right. I came to that conclusion immediately after being fired."

6. **Come to terms with family and friends.** Humor helps us resolve conflict and create bonds with those closest to us. A friend of mine changed her will to read, *"I leave my relatives all the money they owe me!"* They say the reason grandparents and children get along so well is that they have *"time"* as a common enemy. The children have too much ahead and the grandparents have too little left.

7. **Have fun.** Having fun is a question of attitude. Any mistake that does not hurt has in it the element of humor. *A teacher asks a student; "If you had 50 cents in one pocket and 75 cents in another, what would you have?" The student responds with delight, "Someone else's pants!"*

8. **Overcome failure.** You have to believe you have failed before you can become a failure. Sure, others such as teachers and coaches may tell you when you have made mistakes, but all of us make mistakes. Edison failed thousands of times before he succeeded in developing the electric light bulb. One man who had been repeatedly unsuccessful at establishing a lasting relationship said, "It seems I keep discovering all the things that don't work. I'm the Edison of relationships, only instead of filaments, I've gone through people!" It takes only one success to overcome all the failures.

9. **Learn to be patient.** There is an adage, "All things come to one who waits." Traffic tests my patience. *I cannot understand why they call stalled, bumper-to-bumper traffic "rush hour."* Sometimes I find humorous music, a radio talk show or put in a

humorous cassette. All of these things use humor to teach me to be more patient.

10. **Regain self-esteem.** Learning to laugh at yourself and your mistakes is a wonderful way to enhance your self-esteem. Through developing self-acceptance, we can in turn accept others more easily. Humor gives us the space to discover that it's okay to be human and imperfect and to extend that understanding to others.

11. **Handle endings.** Terminating relationships can be difficult. But, using humor to replace the lost relationship is good mental health. One woman's husband joined a monastery after their divorce, leaving her with the responsibilities of raising a family on her own. She once said, *"After he had me, the only place left to turn was God."* Her humor helped her cope with a difficult and challenging situation.

The Eventual Use of Humor

I am often asked where all these uses of humor and comedy lead? For me, the ultimate experience is being a clown. Clowns immerse themselves in all aspects of humor and comedy. The clown is a comic, the visual image of humor and incorporates all kinds of antics including magic, puppets, mime, skits and drama. Clowns use humor and comedy in parades, circuses, hospitals, churches, shopping malls and the home. To be a clown is to be mature in your appreciation that humor and comedy is much more than being silly. Anyone can develop the skills to become a successful clown. The most necessary requirement in becoming a clown is the willingness to bring joy and happiness to others. Becoming a clown really starts with that attitude.

Being a clown does not appeal to everyone. But, if the idea intrigues you, the first step toward becoming a clown is to contact a clown in your area. As a clown, you start with a comical face and costume. A proper face and costume can best be achieved by joining up with another clown or clowns for advice and suggestions. Following are three major, international clown networks which are easy to contact and who will be happy to refer you to a clown in your area.

1. Clowns of America International
    P.O. Box Clown, Richeyville, PA 15358-0532.
    (888) 52-Clown
    http://www.coai.org

2. World Clowns of America /
    WCA Administrator's Office
    P.O. Box 77236, Corona, CA 92877-1017
    (800) 336-7922
    http://www.worldclownassociation.com

3. Clowns International
    30 Sandpiper Close, Marchwood,
    Southampton, Hants, S040 4XN, England
    023 8087 3700
    www.clowns-international.co.uk

Getting involved with another clown or a clown club (called "alleys") is the key to becoming a successful clown. Take your time. Visit, ask questions and observe the kinds of support they offer. Becoming a clown is a social experience. You share with your fellow clowns (called "Joeys") the endless funny situations that continually arise.

If you've decided to try out clowning, the first thing to determine is what kind of a clown you want to become. The house of clowning has many mansions. Caring clowns work in hospitals. Clown ministry works with faith development. Maybe you would like to become a performing artist such as a magician, juggler, comic, mime or balloon sculptor. Some clowns become specialists in puppetry. Other clowns work in schools or in mental health facilities. Many clowns just relax and enjoy volunteering. The avenues are endless and the rewards are fantastic.

The first step in defining your personality as a clown is to create your costume. For this, you may want to select a costumer. Costumers are great at designing a costume to fit your personality, while keeping within the strict guidelines of proper fashion and style. Look through some pictures of clowns. Your clown club will most likely have a library from which you may borrow videos and other material. If possible, find a costumer in your local area who is recommended by two or more other clowns.

In addition to your costume, you define your clown personality with your face. Your mentor clown or clown club will offer instruction and is ever changing as you grow and mature as a clown. An interesting phenomenon experienced by most clowns is what I refer to as an "alternate identity." An alternate identity is like a mantle you take on, a whole other personality, somewhat separate from yourself. My wife says it's like being married to two people. A husband said to me that his wife appeared more uninhibited when dressed as a clown.

Another phenomenon of clowning takes place with those "chronologically enhanced." As a clown, others see you as younger and treat you less formally. Children and adults talk more to you as part of their group. You realize that, over the years, formal and polite treatment had a way of making you feel distanced from others. As a clown, others treat you more inclusively. As a clown, you are "one of the family."

What Happens Next?

Look at the various activities in which the clowns in your area are involved. With a "buddy clown," tag along and explore the activities that look most inviting. Note the skills involved. Some clowns become so enthusiastic they "bite off more than they can chew." Take your time! Start with some simple tricks, a few basic balloon sculptures and some questions. You might ask the children what their favorite subject in school is or what happened on their vacation or birthday. You soon become comfortable handling different situations such as the child who says, "You aren't really a clown." or the child that wants you do something beyond your training.

Bringing It All Together

While clowning is an activity that uses all kinds of comedy and humor, the power of humor to improve our lives starts with the simple enjoyment of the humor all around us. To get the most out of humor means to know what it is and to understand how it works. Arriving at a definitive use of humor is a never-ending process. But there are certain milestones marking the way:

Step 1: Recognize that you can personally benefit by increasing the use of humor in your life.

Step 2: Develop the ability to observe and use the humor that permeates the world in which you live.

Step 3: Learn what kinds of humor you like from others and develop the basic skills for sharing this humor.

Step 4: Have a strong desire to bring joy and happiness into the lives of others.

Step 5: Make a life long commitment to continually educate yourself to the new discoveries that humor brings to you and those whom you love.

I think a person has "arrived":
- When humor enables you to love life and living.

- When you find that your tolerance for the transgressions and omission of others has increased.

- When you make friends easily.

- When you feel safe and you sincerely care about the welfare of others.

These are truly the rewards of using humor.

Doodle Here

Chapter 3

Humor in Education
Or, Are Teachers from Mars and Students from Snickers?

"Thank you son, clowning is a learning
process and your criticisms help."

Chapter 3 assumes that the only constant thing in life is change. Education enables us to adjust. Humor enables us to:

1. Enjoy educating ourselves and others.

2. Open new opportunities.

3. Apply humor and comedy as part of learning and teaching in educational institutions.

Chapter 3

Humor in Education
Or,
Are Teachers from Mars and
Students from Snickers?

Humor is more important than knowledge.

– Albert Einstein

While my class of 27 fifth grade students was attending an art class I had only 45 precious minutes to grade papers, review lesson plans and revise classroom displays. *"Principal Dodson wants to see you in his office"* *the classroom intercom blared. Arriving at Mr. Dodson's* *office I sat next to a 3rd grade boy who was obviously in* *trouble. The boy snuggled up next to me with his head down.* *Softly he questioned; "Are you in trouble too?"* It's a fine line between teaching and learning. Having worked much of my life in the field of education as an administrator, I learned more from my students and staff than I taught.

One of my most challenging tasks was while I had the privilege of serving as Principal for the Singapore American School in Southeast Asia. It was my job to implement a new educational model for expatriate students entitled "Individually Guided Education." We had received three million dollars to create a cutting-edge model that catered to the individual needs of each student.

Once we had our program in place, some 23 dignitaries, representing professional educators from England, Canada, Australia and the United States, came to study and evaluate our program. A great deal of excitement and preparation went into receiving these dignitaries. Classrooms were meticulously cleaned, students and teachers were briefed, tables were set and supporting documentation compiled. As this assemblage of representatives was escorted from the orientation meeting in the cafeteria to the classrooms, a staff person ran up and whispered in my ear, "We can't have a first-class, model school when there is no toilet paper in the ladies' lavatories." In our rush to polish our image for presentation, we had overlooked a rather small, yet essential, detail. Although it was embarrassing, I also found it ironic — a harmless "mistake" easily rectified. I was actually grateful for that brief moment of humor, because it acted as a reprieve from the stress of that morning's activities.

As an educator, I've witnessed first hand how humor helps us learn. When an instructor smiles and assures her student, it reduces tension and embarrassment. Humor can also diffuse confrontation. A teacher suspecting her student of lying can say that George Washington was a great man who admitted telling a falsehood. Other techniques include humorous games that focus on a process rather than the product and can pull the rug out from under students' competition for control.

Unfortunately, some professional educators become so immersed in the structure and limitations of theory that they overlook the practical realities of life. The following is a good example. Once I was racing across the playground to aide a child who had fallen from a swing and was screaming in pain.

Teacher, "Jane Carlon" came sprinting across the field to intercept me. "Mr. Wheeler!" she yelled. I stopped. "Mrs. Carlon," I questioned, "What is it?" To my amazement, Mrs. Carlon huffed, "I cannot possibly give the Iowa Test of Basic Skills with only #1 leaded pencils. We need #2 to complete the test." Jane was oblivious to the injured child. My concern was not with pencils, but with a fallen child.

As a school administrator I know to listen for a "sense of humor" when hiring. It is a joy to know that the best teacher has a sense of humor. Trust me! When dealing with people, the premiere rule is, "Do not sacrifice the practical realities of life and living for educational theory." When you are open to accept the spontaneous appearances of humor when helping people learn, you allow them to harness that light-hearted energy to create a wide range of benefits for themselves and others.

Humor and education have one strong point in common. They are both highways of information allowing you to travel in two directions. Humor can help us learn through lightening our hearts. Even games act as "mirthful" ways to learn. Games like Checkers or Chess help us learn to focus. Music is believed to help in math because both deal in proportion. Humorous stories provide enthusiasm and the confidence necessary for reading. The other gift of humor is the ability to share humor with others. Humor opens up an opportunity to educate and still be an interactive part of society. The purpose of this chapter is to show how humor can help us learn and help us teach, in our daily lives as well as in formal settings.

Humor Helps Us Learn

Humor is a great communication tool. It allows us to handle concerns more effectively. Arriving at the airport, I discovered my flight had been cancelled. By joshing with the ticketing agent I learned additional details about connecting flights. Much of this information was volunteered because I chose to use humor rather than anger. Humor opens up topics for discussion. Selective use of humor gives people the sense that you are on top of things, that you are able to cope and that you are open to them and their ideas.

Practice your humor skills! As you try different humorous techniques and tactics, be sensitive to how others react. Try out new jokes or different approaches to humor. As you become more proficient, you'll find that people will share information with you because they are comfortable with you. This is a side effect of your ability to use humor. Through sharing your sense of humor, you help others relax around you; they're more likely to drop their protective shields.

As you understand your own sense of humor better, you can use it consciously to defuse helplessness. Humor helps you approach sensitive topics yet back away before feelings get hurt. Humor facilitates creativity in problem solving helping us "think outside of the box." In this way, humor helps to keep our minds open to solutions that ordinarily might not otherwise occur to us.

Here's an example:

· · ·

· · ·

· · ·

In the diagram above, connect nine dots in four straight lines without lifting your pencil from the paper. Can't see it? Take a moment and tell yourself a joke, or think of something humorous, then try again. You can only solve this problem by thinking outside of the "box" of dots. (For the answer, see the solution at the end of this chapter, on page 92.)

You can use humor to be a successful student by delivering "content plus entertainment." Including appropriate humor in your writing and oral presentations will create interest and provide a "resting spot" for your audience. When preparing a report, vary the pace, get the reader involved and tell stories. If you are giving an oral report, use visual aids. Remember, learning is like anything else in life and when you get right down to it, we have to do it for ourselves, and humor helps you communicate effectively.

The rest of this chapter deals with utilizing humor as a teacher or speaker in more formally structured settings. Those readers who work as professional educators, or who work within fields that require skills in presenting materials and information to groups, will find the following helpful in learning how to harness the power of humor.

The Playful Teacher

Most of the best teachers I have known introduce an element of playfulness in addition to establishing respect and responsibility. Some examples of this might be a history teacher who comes to school dressed in a costume illustrative of the era being discussed, playing an eminent character from the past. Another example is the elementary teacher who removed all the chairs and desks from the classroom and replaced them with cushions and used colorful texts as reference materials, allowing students to gain and share knowledge in a relaxed, risk-free environment. I knew a college professor who dressed up as a clown in order to give his students a visual model of irrational humor. By collecting stories, anecdotes and witty sayings, the best teachers have an arsenal of humor

Around 1776 an Italian Captain set sail under secret orders. He became lost at sea. Spotting a British Admiralty ship, he signaled for help. "Where are you from?" asked the Admiral. "I cannot say," responded the Italian. "Well, where are you going?" questioned the Admiral. Again, the Captain responded, "I cannot say." "If you do not know where you are from nor where you are going," said the Admiral in disgust, "it hardly matters where you are," and he sailed away. Just like the Italian Captain, you must know where you are with your students and where you want them to go, otherwise your students have no sense of direction. A rule of thumb is to say what you are going to teach — teach — then review what was taught in terms of what is coming up next.

Knowing where you are with your skills of educating, and knowing what kind of an educator you want to become, keeps you from becoming lost as a professional educator. Every teacher has a plan. However, things don't always happen the way you expect. A storm comes up — challenging the teacher to incorporate the storm into her teaching. An earthquake in another community provides opportunity to write, read and discuss. Fire engines going by can draw students to the window. Do you have an alternative plan? To become the very best teacher is to keep your options open so that the unexpected events contribute to learners rather than act as a distraction.

Knowing when to be humorous can depend upon how sensitive you are to the concerns and issues facing your learners. Do you stop and ask the students their ideas and perceptions? Do you restate questions and comments to show that you are hearing what they say? How well prepared are you to include humor in alternative programs? Are you truly knowledgeable about the subject? How can you incorporate humor revealed in that late-breaking news item or article in a journal? Humor can suggest enthusiasm. How would you rate your level of enthusiasm? How available and helpful are you to your students? Humor can suggest empathy. To become the very best teacher is to become a caring teacher. Students do not care how much you know unless they know how much you care.

Humor in Teaching Children

Preschool children laugh 300 to 400 times a day. Adults laugh seven to 15 times a day. Why? As we grow up, do we lose a lot of playfulness in our lives? I share with other school administrators the observation that as children become more preoccupied with competition and acceptance, laughter and playfulness diminish. During this same period of time enthusiasm and playfulness outside of school activities remain buoyant. It is generally understood that this occurs because students perceive being successful as students with being serious.

Children practice attitudes and behaviors that are modeled by adults. If teachers approach learning as fun, often the children find learning fun. Children's enjoyment of humor provides them with a sense of competency. Humor bolsters self-esteem because it gives the child an opportunity to try out thoughts and ideas without risking being wrong. Humor helps creates a sense of positive identity by copying adult humor in play activities. Teasing or parody can reduce the situation to the point of laughter. Teasing, however, should be used with great discretion and only in a friendly tone.

Humor is appropriate for young children because they have an innate appreciation for incongruity (when two things do not agree, the "what's wrong with this picture?" model). A girl pretending to comb her hair with a pencil, a cat saying, "moo" are examples of incongruity. Children (and some lucky adults) love laughing at something that doesn't make sense.

One school I know has consciously chosen to harness the power of laughter in their educational setting. Fifth and sixth graders at Frazer School in Canton, Ohio are encouraged to use laughter. These sessions include a series of stretching exercises and "laugh exercises" which usually dissolve into giggling. Older students who have mastered the exercises are encouraged to teach the second-graders. The school states that this program of laughter has promoted creativity, reduced stress, helped develop leadership skills and has fostered an element of fun in the educational process.

St. Albert School in Dearborn Heights near Detroit, Michigan tried an experiment. The principal gathered the entire school in the gym, where they laughed and giggled like a gaggle of geese. The mirth was carefully engineered. They did not tell jokes but practiced different laughing styles. They did a "He-He, a Ho-Ho and a Ha-Ha-Ha" The children readily accepted the exercises. They were experiencing a sense of freedom not previously associated with school. The program gave the kids a good laugh even though there was nothing funny to laugh about.

In order to learn, children must feel a desire or need to learn. Laughing helps create a desire to learn. As educators, we must first give them the "pay-off" so they will anticipate the learning event with a positive attitude. Humor helps us do this. Humor enables the learning environment to be friendly and safe. Humor develops trust between children and adults, which in turn, creates the atmosphere of safety for a child. Humor conveys the message that you genuinely enjoy the child's company. Children like to participate in the learning when it relates to their world. Fun is part of a child's' world. For example, say you are teaching social skills. Suggest that they have a "party." Invite them to determine what kind of party they want. What will they need to create that? Can you afford the costs? Build upon the child's previous experiences with parties.

Sometimes, children will try to exert control over adults by engineering power struggles. For example, a child might claim in the classroom, "Dad said I could." You find out later that Dad said nothing of the kind. When confronted, the child responds, "I was only kidding." "Right," you chidingly respond, "The answer is no, and I am not kidding."

Playing improvisation games is an effective method for stepping outside the loop of power struggles initiated by children against authority. Improvisation is spontaneous and softens the borders of control by acknowledging your own vulnerability. It's relatively safe because there are no mistakes in improvisation; you don't have to think about what you will do or anticipate what others are going to do. The only rule is that you agree to accept any reality offered within a structure and commit to that reality without a moment's hesitation. I call one of my favorite improvisations "The Situation." "The Situation" allows maximum creativity. A person or small group identifies the "Situation." This can be anything involving humans, animals, plants or inanimate objects such as rocks, doors or furniture. Situations come from the family, school social gatherings or the environment. Objects or people can be from any time: past, present or future. A situation might involve conversations between a rock and a chair, two dinosaurs, a planet and a sun, or a deer and a wolf. The opportunities for creativity, as well as spontaneous humor, are unlimited. There are only three rules:

1. The safety of all participants is of primary importance.

2. There must be mutual consent between those involved and the "authority".

3. Any participant can stop the improvisation by saying, "STOP."

The improvisation ends with a discussion of impressions and general observations in terms of the objectives of the curriculum.

Humor is an important feature of peer communication and relationships. The use of puns and riddles helps develop social skills. For example, *"Why did the dinosaur cross the road?" Answer: "Because chickens hadn't yet evolved."* Or, *"Why did the boy throw the butter out the window?" Answer: "He wanted to see the butterfly."* This kind of dialogue allows experimentation in communication without exposing the child's ego. Humor can "prime" your students' brains for problem solving and improve their performance. Humor is considered a sign of intelligence. You need to "know" so you can communicate the ambiguity, incongruity using humor.

Reducing the Stress of Evaluation

I knew something was wrong. Two weeks before the end of the school term my son started to become very quiet and sullen. Sure enough, he had three low grades. Worse still, they were in math, science and social studies. As parents we wanted confrontation. Instead we reduced the tension by saying that things can only get better. The family formed a support team. We, with our son, had a conference with the teachers. We kept the conversation light and positive focusing on positive resolution. Could he do make-up work? How can we support at home? Does the school or teacher have email? What rewards could we give our son for upgrading his performance? We set up a strategy to follow up keeping track of his performance and aware of what was coming next. Not only did his grades improve, but his enjoyment of learning increased.

Evaluation can create stress. First, the process of evaluation places judgment on what the students have learned by someone who might appear to have absolute control over their lives. Second, this same process subjectively evaluates how well they have learned without consideration that each learner is "special." An evaluation may differ between teachers who teach the same subject. Evaluation tends to be a stressful experience. Most evaluations are given in written form. You can add a drawing of two hands shaking, a sweating head, or an apple with a smiling face can indicate approval. A finger pointing or a light bulb might suggest importance. An angry face or a sleeping head on a pillow might suggest areas needing improvement. The use of "cartoons, stickers or school district 'clip-on' humor" can be used as part of the written test and it tends to ease stress. Humor gives you and your students an avenue for significantly reducing stress-filled evaluations.

Because evaluation is an ongoing process, you can start your evaluation by assessing existing skills and information at the beginning of the program. Play activities enable both learner and instructor to evaluate where they are in terms of expectations. Inject into written evaluations a joke, bits of humor or a cartoon that let your students know that mistakes make us human and education is a form of self-forgiveness.

Students are more at ease when levels of expectation are within their grasp. If you are teaching students about humor, you might say, "Tomorrow, I want you to bring to class one example of humor you have observed." (For an example of a student contribution, see the illustration titled "Your Ideas" that follows.on page 78). Setting a standard that might appear ridiculously easy can be a good thing because success, no matter how simple, builds confidence and inspires students to take risks. Rewards for achievement will reinforce learning throughout your program. Good results are the direct result of good communication. Insert humor into your educational forms. Humor lets the students know that to make mistakes is human and can be part of the growing process.

At the conclusion of the program thank the learners and give them an opportunity to evaluate the course. (For an example of humorous feedback, see illustration titled

- -

> **Your Ideas:**
> _____
> _____
> _____
> _____
> _____
> _____
> _____
> _____
> _____
>
> **Comments:**
> _____
> _____
> _____

"What Did You Think? on page 79). You can prepare a narrative evaluation form or a multiple choice or rating feedback form. These selections should be easy to understand, open-ended and not time consuming. For example, "What did you like best about this course?" or, "Rank this course from 0 to 10 with 0 being the best score." I always like to wear something amusing on days when evaluations are taking place. I have a shirt with clown faces on it. You can collect buttons with witty sayings and quotations.

Humor in Teaching Adults

Obviously, teaching adults is vastly different from teaching children. First, adults have a background of varied experiences to draw from. As an educator, you need to find out if any of this background affects what it is you are going to teach. If you are teaching some innovative ways to cook,

What Did You Think..

Please complete this form by circling the image that best expresses your feelings.

1. What Impact did the presentation have on you?

☺   ☺   ☹   💣   ☠

2. Were you impressed with the material?

☺   ☺   ☹   💣   ☠

3. Was the information easy to understand?

☺   ☺   ☹   💣   ☠

4. Did you obtain information you can use?

☺   ☺   ☹   💣   ☠

Comments?

_____
_____
_____

and you have five professional cooks as part of your learning group, you would do well to incorporate them into your presentation. Their presence might change a one-man presentation into a panel or symposium focusing interactively on your topics.

Whether you're teaching children or adults, however, the best place to start is by setting measurable objectives.

Ask yourself what it is that you want these people to be able to do at the end of this presentation which they were unable to do at the beginning. If you find that your students can run 75 meters, set 100 meters as a goal. One hundred meters is something you can see and easily measure. Another way to do this is through assessment. Prepare a questionnaire or just ask a simple question. Let's say that you are teaching a class on using a computer and the Internet to send and receive E-mail. You might open the first session with the question, "Do any of you have any experience with E-mail?" Now you have pre-established a set of computer skills you want them to know. You can use humor in the form of jokes, cartoons, lists, a story or a handout to both assess where your learners are in terms of the topic and, set the stage for learning. By pre-testing your learners, you can adjust the material to your audience. Now you're ready for the next level.

All learners like to be independent. While children have to be dependent because they are vulnerable, adults see independence as part of their sense of identity. Within reasonable bounds, treat all contributions as "good" and all learners as valuable participants. Let's say you're presenting a new technique to a group. One student in your group states, "We have always done it this other way." Rather than argue or defend your position for change, remember that sometimes suggesting change can create a strong resentment. Avoid confrontation as this will most likely lead to a power struggle in which neither educator nor learner wins. Instead, provide the learner with an opportunity to succeed. Lets' say you're facilitating a cooking class. One learner has had a negative experience with one of the ingredients you're including in this lesson.

The solution is to acknowledge her experience, and offer her a chance at a new technique that might well override it. Use humor to engage her in experiencing something different from what she knows. Keep it light and fun. She can take part in the preparation of the meal, and share in the success and praise of the finished product. Success overrides the threat of change and can suspend disbelief based on previous experiences. Humor through facial expressions and body language practiced in front of a mirror in private then video taped in the classroom is a wonderful way to show your students how much fun they can have discovering new points of view.

In addition, many adult learners have preoccupations that interfere with what they are learning. Family problems, poor diet, traffic problems; all are opportunities to stray from the presentation. These issues can steal audience attention and engagement. **This is a perennial challenge: you can excite some of the learners some of the time, but it's sure hard to excite all of the learners all of the time. Be mindful of the pacing of your presentation so you can forestall monotony. Change pace by involving the learners in questions-and-answer sessions, stop talking and draw or diagram: invite contributions from the learners: bring up controversial issues — or simply change your body language (if you are standing, move around the room).** If you have to impart facts, use humor to keep the energy of your audience at a higher level. The sound of laughter rippling through a crowd energizes and relaxes everyone — including the teacher.

Some students carry "extra baggage" such as fear of indignity, resentment of authority or worry. Now, all learners worry: there isn't much you can do about this except to be aware. Take a little extra time and make your audience feel comfortable. Again, humor is a great tool to help learners relax. Building an arsenal of humor to use during your teaching role is not difficult. When you hear something funny at a meeting or on TV, jot it down. Build on your own, humorous experiences and share them: people prefer humor based on true experiences over canned jokes. Assure your listeners that everyone's part of the same team and that your role is to support them and not to judge or criticize. Within reasonable bounds, let them see your own vulnerabilities, the human side of your personality. Share your story, your family and your failures, but use humor to keep it light.

Being an effective communicator starts with a positive, confident attitude. From this foundation you can insert humor to make what you are presenting a memorable experience. **Come up with a snappy title that gets the learners attention.** Reduce your content to five statements or fewer. Go through your material ahead of time and identify "key words" such as "Do not eat poison," "Gear up for change" or "Guess who is boss?" Next, explore exciting ways to present your information. Explore different A/V styles such as overhead projectors, videos, charts and graphs. Vary the tone, pitch and rhythm of your voice: consider including role-playing or open discussion topics. Don't forget questioning strategies, audience participation and input groups.

Then, review your content to see where you can throw in some humorous questions; ask a question or call for a response. "How many of you think this is correct?" "How many of you think something else is correct?" There are questions that have humor because they are relevant. "How many of you have a pet dog?" "How many of you have a pet chicken?" "How many of you like chocolate?" You can use exaggerated outrageous and ridiculous examples in class. Lastly, remember the basic "three" of all presentations: 1) Tell them what it is you're going to say, 2) say it, and 3) tell them what you just said. It's not redundant — it's thorough.

Setting the Stage

Setting the stage is similar to decorating. When you decorate a room you establish an overall "tone." It is the most important act in teaching and learning because it also sets the tone and helps the learners predict what is going to take place. Three of the most important factors in learning are, 1) relevance, 2) relevance and 3) relevance. You must start by learning about your audience. One of my favorite activities is to select cartoons relating to the subject I'm teaching. I remove the captions and ask the students to create their own captions. Individually, or in small groups, I have them share their creations. In this way, they teach me something about themselves and how they learn as well as their kind of "funny bones". Discuss the results, connecting some of the captions they've created to your presentation. Or, simply ask the students to share something personal. Choose a relatively "safe" topic such as the most humorous, exciting, adventuresome or momentous events in their lives.

Activities excite the learner and reinforce learning. Activities that are fun are especially memorable. Here are some "ice-breaker" activities: You enter the room saying loudly "ho-ho, ha-ha-ha" clapping your hands in rhythm. Your audience immediately starts imitating your behavior, which is reinforced by a bright smile and an increase in pace. Having gotten their attention, divide the group into small groups of not more than six. Have each participant tell the funniest thing that has happened to him or her. Someone in each group ends by summarizing the shared experiences. Such activities use humor to establish rapport and bond students into a cohesive learning group.

Using Humor in Presentations

All students, regardless of age or background, learn more effectively when you change the pace. Make an equipment list: overhead projector and screen, needed extension cords, microphone, television and audio players, white board with colored markers, paper supplies and name tags. Vary how you are going to present your information. In advance of your presentation, prepare slides, photographs, charts and graphics that color, characterize and clarify your information. Better yet, provide objects they can feel and see. Remember, learners like to do things other than listen. There are times when a lecture is the best or only appropriate way to teach. If you are requiring your group to listen because it is the only way you can communicate, make sure your information is easy to understand and use humor to extend the attention span of those you're talking to.

Sprinkling humor liberally throughout your presentation not only extends listener's attention but helps change the focus. You can use humorous examples to make it clear why your subject is important and how this learning experience is going to make the student's lives better. Use skits or dramatization; add music if you like. Games formatted like Jeopardy, Who Wants to Be a Millionaire or Weakest Link, can be the basis for a lot of humor and learning in almost any setting.

Assign creative and humorous homework to enhance the learning experience. The newspaper is a marvelous resource. If your topic is humor, have the learners find humorous mistakes in the newspaper or on billboards and road signs. Television is another resource. Pre-identify a relevant source of material on T.V. and have students view and report on their findings.

A close cousin to homework is sharing. A simple form of sharing is to ask your learners a question. You can draw from something they have just learned or from their personal experiences. You might ask them how they deal with traffic, the electronic world of communications or some other frustration. You can divide your learners into small groups and give each group a "problem" to solve. Have each group select a leader to report their solution. Compliment and comment on the material offered.

· ·

Periodically summarize information. A good way to do this is to group the information around a common word that has no more than five letters. For example, let us say you have been teaching the importance of using humor to teach. You have taught them how to provide a positive atmosphere (Relaxation), the constructive use of humorous materials (Interest), rewarding learners (Success) and the importance of taking chances (Experience). When you put the first letter of each of these principles together, they spell the word "RISE." You get the idea; you can do this with virtually any kind of subject matter.

Reinforcement is the final phase of the presentation. Repetition is the most common, yet certainly a poor way, to gain retention. Educators commonly lose all that they have built up by dull and tedious reinforcement activities. Play activities can create reinforcement with a lasting, positive effect on learners. Math, spelling or subject area Bingo is a good example of play reinforcement. Some instructors make up question cards with answers on the back. Students randomly choose a card for the groups to compete for the best answer.

Another type of reinforcement is play activity which fits most situations, and is what I call "Setting the Stage." The instructor "sets the stage," which might be an interview, sales pitch, teacher-and student, customer service or performing a skill. It is important that you clearly explain the circumstances in advance of the activity and, of course set any guidelines such as safety, consideration of other players, timing, etc. After the activity, have the players' share their reactions. Make no judgment calls, but ask the remaining students for their comments. Feel free to fill in any areas that appear incomplete. Continue these activities until you are convinced your students have a solid under-standing of the material.

Another area for reinforcement play is board games. I often take a common game such as Monopoly and reconstruct it, so that it fits the subject matter. Games are great for technical data. You can set up a series of problems that have only one correct answer. You might consider Bingo as a game. In Bingo the answers are available on Bingo cards. The first person to get a straight line receives an award. You can use card games for the same purpose.

There are times when you want to "WOW" your audience. Let's say you want an audience of Sunday School teachers to understand the difference between using illusion and using magic when teaching their students. The difference is that the use of "illusion" can enhance learning, while the use of "magic" can create confusion and frustration. For example: You are teaching the power of Jesus healing. You use a magic trick to illustrate Jesus raising Lazarus from the dead. The use of magic might teach the children that Jesus's healing powers were magic. To avoid this from happening teach that Jesus did not do magic, then demonstrate your point. The following example illustrates this point:

"You talk casually to your audience. Then you bring out a deck of cards and ask one of the teachers to volunteer and draw any card. The volunteer draws the card and shows it to the rest of your audience. The volunteer then slips it randomly back into the deck. You pull out a card and ask the volunteer if this is the card. Your audience is astonished, for it is the exact card. The "magic" created confusion. At this point, you show your audience that all 52 cards are the same."

By revealing the secret, you taught your audience that the "illusion" kept their rapt interest but left as a magic trick where the "secret" was not shared, the same experience had the potential to create confusion. A visual and interactive demonstration of any point you are making to an audience will always be more memorable than merely telling them something.

• •

Teaching as a Clown

We see clowns as silly people who entertain children. The idea that clowns can teach or help us heal is a new concept in our modern world. Becoming a "clown teacher" is to become a creative and playful teacher. Playful and creative teachers are teachers who care. For me, acting as a clown teacher has been one of the most rewarding experiences of my teaching career.

Becoming a clown teacher is not hard. In all of us there is a "clown" suppressed from childhood. Remember how silly your older brother or sister was when talking to a love interest on the phone? Do you remember getting the "giggles" and not being able to stop? The clown in all of us, even if suppressed, will still tend to assert its presence at unexpected times. To become a clown teacher, you simply need to rebuild your strengths in humor that you may have set aside as an adult. To do this, start a logbook where you record funny events from the past as well as humorous things you come across during the day. For each of these funny moments, write down what it was, when it happened and what made it funny to you. After a time, you will see a pattern emerge. Perhaps you are laughing during meal times, when you're in a crowd, or entertained by television, radio or video. Label this pattern. Labeling this pattern is a great way to discover a name for the clown in you that is trying to express itself. If you are laughing every time you hear a frog croak you might call yourself "Ribbitz." I call myself "Muggins," because I laugh softly inside, rather than laughing with a boisterous belly laugh. To me, "Muggins" is a soft sounding name.

We have no problem seeing clowns as being somewhat "different". Being a clown teacher entails the use of costume, face and language (called "patter") to bring joy and laughter to learners. The clown teacher is different from an ordinary teacher in that the clown can do things and say those things that many educators feel would compromise the "integrity" of their professionalism as an educator. The "professional" may worry about "loss of discipline" if seen as humorous or clowning, but the clown teacher has more leeway. Suppose you are teaching a child the value of a number less than one. You have your cutouts, including a whole circle (representing a whole number one), and then a half circle (representing one-half of a whole) and a quarter circle, and so on. The teacher might incorporate humor in this demonstration by putting a smiley face painted on the whole number, a half a smiley face on the half, and so on. The clown can extend this humor by incorporating the use of nonsense to demonstrate the same points. The clown can become the character of the whole number, then drop to his knees for the half, and so on through the divisions, bringing a "cartoon" effect to the learning process. Being silly and using nonsense is expected from the clown. All teachers are encouraged to use "play" as part of the teaching process, but the clown can participate like a child and with a child, in play activities.

Clowns can alter costume and dress to create a point. Clowns can dress up as a punctuation mark. The clown can conduct the students in making noises that signify a punctuation mark while reading aloud. The beloved Victor Borge used audible punctuation as one of his routines. (A tape of his performance should still be available.) Within reasonable bounds, it is permissible for the child to participate in physical comedy with the clown. The students can clap, or laugh or make silly sounds. The clown teacher can expand the boundaries of learning experiences beyond that of the regular teacher.

The relationship between the student and the clown teacher goes well beyond the limitations of a regular teacher. The student is more "risk-free" with the clown teacher. The negative and threatening aura of "evaluation" is significantly reduced with the clown teacher. In addition, the threat of discipline is nearly extinguished, because the clown and the learner are collaborating in the learning experience. The child is free to explore and be creative.

The clown teacher is very effective in programs in which a child is sent to the clown for a specific purpose. Their experience with the clown is specific and temporary. In another type of program, the clown teacher comes into the learning environment. This might be as a teaching assistant in the classroom working with a limited number of students. It might be in a multi-level assembly where the clown is putting on a performance that motivates the student to become more involved in reading, science, or a specified subject.

Today's educational environment sometimes entails dealing with children who have histories of abuse or violence and who may bring that negative energy into the classroom. Clowns can be professionally trained to assist in these issues. Humor — and specifically clown humor — may provide a non-threatening method for dealing with the negative feelings.

Clowns can be trained to break through mental barriers. Clowns can be trained to:

• Enable others to accept differences in intelligences, talents and gifts.

• Use magic and puppets to open up communication.

• Take complicated ideas and reduce them to manageable concepts.

• Use role-playing and clown-student interactivity to help others honor diversity.

• Help integrate the concepts of race, creed and gender.

These skills can function both in and out of the instructional program.

Humor, and specifically the use of clown techniques, can be used by educational institutions to help learners:
1. Cope with stress,

2. Increase creativity and problem solving,

3. Facilitate learning,

4. Boost morale, and

5. Help learners develop new insights.

Frequently, when people recall and identify their most influential teacher, one of the top characteristics they cite is the teacher's sense of humor.

Clown teachers can even be "certified." To be certified means that you have studied and passed qualification standards. These standards are uniform and established through institutions of higher learning. That, along with recommendations, sets the teacher aside from the general population, thus commanding just compensation. A clown teacher who has an advanced certification as a "reading specialist" or "librarian" has an even higher value.

One limitation to being a clown teacher is that, in today's economic climate, many public schools lack the funds to pay higher salaries for certified clown teachers. However, once clown teachers have proven themselves as providers of a more specialized or "better" instructional style, compensation is usually adjusted upwards and included in budgeting. Sometimes a little "clowning" goes a long way. The "law of diminishing returns" can set in. This can lead to over exposure. It's like going to a circus: once or twice a year is fun, but every weekend? While it varies from student to student, you can tell when your effect is wearing off. Usually the student starts becoming playful or teasing. This might take the form of such things as playing with your props, squeezing your nose, pulling on your wig or stamping on your shoes. The child is saying that they are ready to move on to something else.

One of the benefits of being a clown teacher, as well as a certified teacher, is the ability to go into private practice as a "tutor." A regular teacher functioning as a tutor often has to deal with the challenges of teaching the "reluctant learner." This is because, when private tutoring is required, the child often feels he or she is being punished; time spent being tutored is often time the child would normally spend playing. The clown tutor, however, doesn't feel like a punishment. Not only does the child look forward to "playing" with a new friend (the clown), but the student may want to invite friends as well. Thus, the clown tutor can charge a higher hourly fee and get just as good or better results.

The clown teacher can earn extra money over and beyond that of working as a teacher. As a clown, you can do birthday parties, fashion shows, company picnics and entertainment routines. Your reputation as a performer enhances your reputation as a teacher. As more and more people learn of you as a clown teacher and tutor, the greater the demand will become for your services as a performer.

Becoming a Clown Teacher

At this point, it is time to find a clown to be your mentor. Surprisingly, there are some eight thousand clowns around the country. To find one in your area contact either:

1. Clowns of America International
    COAI is located at P.O. Box Clown,
    Richeyville, PA 15358-0532.
    (888) 52-Clown
    http://www.coai.org

2. World Clowns of America /
    WCA Administrator's Office

P.O. Box 77236,
Corona, CA 92877-1017
(800) 336-7922
http://www.worldclownassociation.com

3.   Clowns International
     30 Sandpiper Close,
     Marchwood, Southampton,
     Hants, S040 4XN, England
     023 8087 3700
     www.clowns-international.co.uk

You will have an opportunity to work with your own club (called an "alley") or your clown friend, in order to develop your costume and clown face. Once this is accomplished, you are ready to become a clown teacher.

Answer to diagram on page 70:

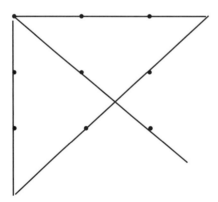

Chapter Four

Humor, Health and Healing

"I'll have an ounce of prevention."

Chapter 4 assumes that humor
and comedy improves health and
healing because humor enables us to:
- Use your mind to help your body.

- Develop ways to help others heal
  and maintain health.

- Understand the professional application of humor and comedy in
  area of health and healing.

Chapter Four

Humor, Health and Healing

*"Humor heightens our sense of survival and
preserves our sanity."*

– Charlie Chaplin

A friend of mine was facing chemotherapy which
would most likely include hair loss. Being meticulous by
nature, she checked to make sure that her insurance
coverage would cover the purchase of a wig. Sure enough,
a few months into treatment, her hair started falling out.
She purchased a wig and filed a claim for reimbursement
with her insurance company. To her surprise, her claim
was denied. She called her insurance carrier for an explanation. The claims agent explained that a wig is not
covered. "But I called in advance and was assured this
would be covered." my friend protested. After several
minutes of being put on hold, the claims agent provided
the following justification "The problem is that you filed
for the wrong thing. Please resubmit your claim for a
cranial prosthesis. Be sure to include a prescription from
your doctor." My friends first reaction was anger. But why
take it out on the insurance clerk? Besides, the situation

was so absurd that laughter was the most sensible response.

The line between anger and joy is razor-thin. Our choices can make the difference between health and illness.

Part of my experience as "Muggins" the clown has been doing volunteer work at a nearby hospital as a "caring clown." My job is to help alleviate suffering whenever possible by providing humor, comfort or just distractions for patients and their families. One day I began visiting Mollie in her private room. Mollie was in her late 50s and dying. Yet Molly was determined to squeeze as much enjoyment as possible from the life that remained to her. This happened to include the presence of a Playgirl magazine in her room.

While I was joshing with her about articles in the daily newspaper, she opened her magazine to the male nude centerfold and insisted that I post it on the wall so she could easily see it from her bed. Although the photo was risqué, the head nurse allowed the poster to be displayed with the provision that the gentleman's genitals be covered. I took a leaf from a plant in the room and pasted it over the questionable anatomy. This worked well for the first few days until the leaf began to wither, revealing what the hospital wanted concealed. Mollie and I laughed as nature took command of the situation.

Regardless of how anyone might feel about Mollie's choice in reading material, the humor we shared brought us closer and truly helped Mollie — who died a few days later. In those last few days, humor took her away from her troubles and made her pain and suffering easier to endure.

Humor makes life worth living. If you had everything you thought you wanted, but had no humor, life would be a dreary reality, indeed. As in the examples of Mollie and my balding friend, humor provides an improved quality of life. Humor allowed them to deal with a world of contradiction and paradox.

• •

We often find ourselves in an impractical, purposeless world, a world where all the rules are broken, where what appears true is false and what appears false is true. We live in so much confusion because much of what should make sense is nonsense, and nonsense is sense. We can use humor and laughter to leave behind hardship and the too cruel realities of sickness and death. The world of humor allows us to survive when all else fails.

Rabbi Earl A. Grollman, D.D, author of Living When a Loved One Has Died, wrote: "When human tragedy becomes overwhelming, humor becomes the all natural do-it-yourself wonder drug." We cannot experience humor and still feel depressed, anxious or angry. In those moments of laughter, negative feelings dissolve.

Nancy was sitting in a chair in her hospital room. Her body had, for all practical purposes, shut down. She was very depressed and had no idea of what to do, so she began rummaging through the uplifting reading material her friends had left in her room. But these well-meaning platitudes just made her feel worse. Then she picked up a book of jokes and humorous short stories flipping the pages until she found a story that interested her. Within a few minutes she was laughing and her energy began to rise. For her, humor helped to distract her attention; allowing her body to begin to heal.

Wellness and humor may be intertwined. Do you suppose they mutually reinforce the individual's movement toward vibrancy, productivity and creativity? I have found that when we nurture our "humorous bone," we become more capable of changing our perspectives and of dealing effectively with the challenges of health and healing. While we can't change the facts of our own infirmities, or the fact that another person is suffering, we have complete control over the way we perceive the situation. When we look around us humor is everywhere. The trick is to find it so that you can begin to use it to improve the quality of your life.

Experience has taught me that humor and laughter are the best ways to face any challenging situation.

Hospitals and other institutions dealing with health issues are beginning to introduce humor as a medical technique. Nancy Thompson of Columbus Ohio works at the James Cancer Hospital. Her job is to work with patients whose ordeals with cancer often leave them feeling hopeless and depressed. She employs humor and techniques that engender laughter to successfully reduce stress and improve the patient's perception of life and living. Another staff member Nurse Florence Dillow uses humor, along with alternative therapies, to help her patients survive chronic illnesses. A study from Indiana State University School of Nursing shows that in addition to the reduction of stress and pain, humor may affect immune function by increasing natural killer cells.

Beverly Brummett of Duke University Medical Center in Durham, North Carolina followed 866 adults with heart disease for about 11 years after they had diagnostic heart tests and found that the cheerful patients had a 20% better survival rate. Interestingly, Brummet's studies showed that constant happiness is not the key; avoiding emotional lows is what is vital to prolonging life. "People could potentially extend their life spans with positive emotions."

You will discover that the health benefits of humor too are varied. All kinds of research is available to help you learn more. Three of my favorite sources are:

- Association for Applied and Therapeutic Humor
  http://www.aath.org

- The Humor Foundation
  Humourfoundation.com.au/

- Clown Interactive Programs
  http://ca.geocities.com/forrest2w

When I surveyed the physical benefits of humor, I found that humor: reduces stress, boosts immunity, distracts pain, decreases anxiety, stabilizes mood, rests and relaxes the brain, maintains home, bolsters moral and increases circulation. It is no wonder that the medical profession is paying more attention to the benefits of humor.

Cardiologist Jerome Fleg of the National Heart, Lung and Blood Institute in Baltimore, Maryland, tracked adults from their twenties into old age. In his study, he found that cheerful people had fewer complaints about chest pain. Steven Locke, of the Harvard Medical School in Boston, points out, "Joyful adults receive more emotional support from friends and family as compared to non-cheerful adults. Support from others is very important in predicting someone's future health." Unhappy, isolated people may be less inclined to take their medicines, to eat healthfully or to exercise, according to internist Mary Whooley of the Veterans Administration Medical Center in San Francisco, who claims, "Symptoms of depression lower a patient's quality of life even more than heart disease."

Imagination Techniques

The line between no-humor and humor lies in attitude. If your attitude is that humor is wrong, then you see very little humor. If your attitude is that humor is good, then you experience humor. It is a question of opening yourself up to accepting humor. One approach to opening yourself up to humor is through the use of imagination. A friend of mine created an imaginary companion, a chimpanzee named Chimpy. Chimpy, who accompanied my friend everywhere, was someone to talk to, to share with and help fend off pain and depression. Another patient created a "magical world" into which she could escape. This world had all the things that reality could not offer her — all the smells, colors, landscapes and stories that her imagination could create. Each of these patients used imagination to restore perspective and establish a healthy connection between themselves and their caregivers.

Not all humor is riotous laughter. In fact, an imaginative "warming" of your outlook, without any laughter at all can nevertheless move you from mild depression or lethargy into a positive mood. Say it's a dreary evening and you're exhausted from the rigors of a stressful day. Let's do the following exercise:

Turn down the lights and turn off any commercial background noise such as the TV or radio. Find a comfortable chair and sit in it with your back pressed softly against the back of the chair. Close your eyes and focus on the soothing darkness. Breathe softly, slowly and deeply. Rub your hands together until your palms feel tingly and warm. Place your warm hands gently over your closed eyes, barely touching your eyelids.

As you feel the warmth penetrate your eyes, create a picture from nature; a field of tall grass blowing softly in the wind, a stream meandering brightly through a forest of trees and ferns, a beautiful, vibrant sunset or a full moon nestled amongst silver threaded clouds. Without removing your hands, open your eyes and look at the landscape you just created. Be aware of all its beauty. Go over every detail of this landscape as though you were going to paint this picture on a canvas. Slowly bring the feeling of this landscape through your eyes to inside your head. Let this wonderful, soothing feeling penetrate your entire body from head to toes. Try to merge yourself into the beauty and warmth of the landscape; until you, the landscape and the warmth are one. Be aware of this feeling as you slowly and quietly become aware again of your physical surroundings. Making this exercise part of your daily routine can strengthen your receptivity to joy.

● ●

During the ten years our family lived in the Far East we learned many ways to use imagination to establish a positive mood. For example, try this exercise in concentration. It is similar but more intense. It begins with you seated comfortably in a chair with your eyes closed. Start by breathing in slowly, picture a big smile right between your eyes. Behind this smile, picture a bright red light. Focus on this bright red light with the big smile.

Feel the warmth of the bright red light. Bring this warmth onto your tongue, until it feels warm and you sense the smile and the good feeling this smile gives you. Now slowly move this bright red light with the soft warm smile down towards your heart. Let the red light and warm smile fill up your heart and move slowly through your veins and arteries, throughout your chest and stomach. Embrace this smile, light and warmth, until your entire body is engulfed and aglow. Focus on this feeling until you are completely satisfied. Then, softly and slowly, sensitize yourself again to your surroundings. This kind of concentration exercise can help control your mood and reduce stress.

There are times when you are sick and need to stay home. In such cases, I like to do the following meditation allowing about an hour for the exercise. Turn off the TV and unplug the telephone. In fact, remove all distractions. If you like, light some incense or a candle with the scent of lavender. In this subdued and aromatic atmosphere, sit upright in a comfortable chair. Take long and slow breaths. Relax as much as possible. Take your time. Slowly build an empty sphere of pure vacuum behind your navel — a sphere containing nothing. Allow the sphere to expand and contract as you breathe in and out.

Next, scan your body for any areas that feel hot or distressed. Gather this heat into a bright red ball, which you envision in the middle of your chest. Collect any feelings of impatience, anger or criticism and place them into this hot, red sphere in your chest. Next, allow yourself to become aware of any cold or dark sensations in your body. Collect this cold and darkness — any fear, any sadness — and place it into a deep blue sphere, which you envision in your lower abdomen. Picture this sphere holding all the coldness.

You now have a cold blue sphere in your abdomen, a hot red sphere in your chest, and a sphere of emptiness behind your navel, all at the same time. Now focus on the empty sphere behind your navel and the cold, blue sphere in your abdomen. Bring all the cold from your abdomen up the right side of your body and put it into the vacuum behind your navel. Now focus on the hot sphere in your chest and bring it slowly down the left side of your body and into the vacuum behind your navel. Feel the coldness dissolve the heat until there is no longer any hot or cold. Conclude the exercise by envisioning the vacuum as once again containing nothing and then dissolving. Slowly allow your awareness to return to your surroundings.

Practicing these and other exercises of concentration are ways you can enhance your ability to focus your percep-tions. Finding humor in your environment and experiences is nothing more than shifting your perspectives and percep-tions. Gaining skill at this will allow you to become more proficient at using humor to help you relax, heal and generally enhance your experience of being alive.

During a recent hospitalization a nurse entered my hospital room and removed the thermometer from my mouth. She said my temperature had risen some ten degrees and the doctor was going to order a heavy injection of antibiotics. Since being injected with antibiotics is not a pleasant experience, I pleaded with her to leave me alone for ten minutes. While she was gone I imagined an intense imaginary blue light. I brought this blue light through my head and gradually throughout my body. When she returned, and again took my temperature, it was back to normal astonishing the nurse. My unscientific explanation did not make her feel any better, but, she did not give me the antibiotics, and my recovery continued.

Imagination combines with humor to produce wondrous things. Imagine if you saw bubbles billowing out of a car window you would probably smile, or even chuckle. If you did, you would probably be improving your health. A good chuckle defuses negative emotions such as anger, fear and sadness. Laughter, the body's response to humor, mimics mild exercise. As a result, the level of the stress hormone, cortical, decreases, and mood-enhancing endorphins increase.

Laughter exercises the diaphragm and the abdominal, facial, leg and back muscles. Research states that laughing 100 times is equivalent to a 10-minute workout. It is common to hear that children laugh about 400 times a day, while adults laugh only about 15. Everything about laughter improves the body's ability to get and use oxygen. In addition, laughing makes your blood pressure go down and your muscles relax. You even digest food better and improve your sleep. Why wait? Today is your day to start laughing.

The Fun of Laughter

"Did you hear the one about—-?" Yes, you're about to hear a joke — are you ready to laugh? I once saw a clown do nothing but enter the stage and start laughing. In less than a minute the audience was laughing back without a single joke.

Is laughing contagious? If it is, it is a welcome event because laughter is just plain fun. Here is a different kind of exercise: look at yourself in the mirror and laugh (even if you have to fake the laughter). Go "Ho-Ho" and then "Ha, Ha, Ha." Repeat this several times. It feels odd at first, but you'll soon become comfortable and even enjoy the experience.

Do silly laughs — high, low, Goofy and Three-Stooges. Imitate animals, pig snorts, dog woofs and cat caterwauls. Children love to do this giggling as they create new and exciting sounds. If you feel the need to be a little sensible, you can combine these activities with breathing exercises and stretching — but it's not required.

Try the elephant laugh, where you extend your arm in front of your head like the trunk of an elephant and chortle, imitating a pachyderm. Or the cell phone laughs where you use one hand as a mock phone. As you laugh into the phone, imitate haughty chuckles, different voices and people. Laugh in gibberish or laugh like a ballerina, where you giggle as you twirl like a dancer.

Try a simple laugh of ho, ho, ha, ha, ha, while you clap your hands in rhythm. These may seem silly at first, but they get your energy moving. Wait until you're alone; lock yourself in the bathroom if you have to. Laughing exercises can increase your sense of vitality and shift your mood. The volume and spontaneity of your laughter will create a sudden shift in thought patterns, frequently with hilarious results.

These (and other) exercises are identified by Dr. Kafarians laughter yoga exercises.

Humor and the Chronologically Enhanced

When you stop to think about it, the only time in our lives when we like to get old is when we were children. A friend of mine sent me the following: "You know you are getting older if:

- You once had penny loafers.

- You remember how school paste tastes.

- You know who Edward R. Murrow was.

- You still recall Jack Benny and Allen's Alley.

- "It ain't funny McGee" still makes you laugh.

- Being "Gay" means feeling happy.

- A "fox" is a small, dog-like mammal."

Aging is part of life. While there is nothing we can do to stop it, and little we can do to slow it down, we can change how we live out the aging process. If you want to live a happier, healthier and longer life, try laughing for no reason at all. Simply bug out your eyes, claw at the air with your hands and roar, "ha, ha, ha," until you are laughing uncontrollably. You can hold your arms up over your head and move them up and down in a roller coaster motion, and laugh aloud, as if you were taking a big drop. These kinds of activities work well in the privacy of your home, and even better in groups, because laughter is infectious.

It is said that laughing increases respiration and blood flow to the brain; boosts the immune system, reduces stress and creates a general sense of well-being. Give yourself this test: try to be happy and sad at the same time. Did you find it impossible to do? You can't have two diametrically opposed feelings at the same time. If you're sad and blue, but you still force yourself to laugh, you will improve your state of mind — I guarantee it!

Laughter is a form of play and play helps us stop worrying about what we "coulda, shoulda" be doing. Play is a great way to incorporate humor into our lives, including role playing, dancing and acting. It can include supposedly frivolous games like "20 Questions" and pantomimed, or acting-out games. Even art activities can include this sense of playfulness, as our creations become unintentional masterpieces of absurdity.

When we play, we involve others. Humor enables us to extend our circle of friends. This in turn keeps us in touch with reality and a world filled with humor.

Humor comes from our day-to-day experiences with acceptable mistakes. The elderly are particularly prone to making mistakes. Take the story of Ed, Al and their wives (all elderly) who were playing cards. Ed announced that his memory had gotten so bad that he had recently seen a doctor about the problem. The doctor had given him pills to take. Al spoke up, "I have the same problem. What's the name of the pills he gave you?" Ed looked puzzled for a minute and didn't say anything. Then he brightened up and said, "What's the name of that red flower that has a long stem and thorns?" Al said, "Rose." "Right!" said Ed. Turning to his wife he asked, "Rose, what's the name of those pills I'm taking?" There is humor all around us — we only need to reach out and accept it.

I don't know about you, but I prefer to stick around cheerful friends: the grouches just pull me down. I surround myself with what I love, whether that's family, pets, keepsakes, music, plants, hobbies or whatever. Every day I cherish my health. If it's good, I preserve it. If it's unstable, I focus on improving it.

I love to travel. I travel on cruise ships, tour groups, trips to the mall and family trips. But there is one trip I stay away from, that is the guilt trip. We come on board for the "guilt trip" when we remorse over the things we said and did that can never be changed. How many times do we fail to tell the people we love that we do love them? It happens to everyone at some time or another. So, why "beat yourself up?" It is so easy to take our loved ones for granted. Let humor put a smile on your face. At every opportunity bring joy and happiness through the simple words "I love you." And if you're fortunate enough to spend time with little ones, take full advantage of the opportunity. Having a child fall asleep in your arms is one of the most peaceful feelings in the world. When your newly born grandchild holds your little finger in his little fist, you're hooked for life!

A patient asked his doctor, "Doctor, am I going to die?" "That's the last thing you're going to do," was the doctors reply. Our ultimate concern may be dying but, there is even humor in death and dying. Different cultures around the world have different perspectives about death and dying. Some cultures allow an element of humor. Take the undertakers in Haarlem, a Dutch town, who hire clowns to ease the tension people feel at funerals. The clown's job is to lighten the mood by making children giggle and their parents smile. The funeral clown, Roelof van Wijngaarden says he has already attended three funerals as a clown and the mourners seem to like it. The children start to giggle and their parents get a smile on their faces. "That's what we do; take the tension away." Mr. Van Wijngaarden says — and his tactics include breaking wind loudly! Imagine adults following a coffin to a burial place. Imagine this clown whispering to the children and at the same time letting out a fart. Truth is often stranger than fiction.

Humor Helps Heal the Mind

Humor is beneficial when a person is too close to a problem. For many people, the burden of medical or personal problems becomes onerous and unbearable. Humor helps people to distance themselves, and gain a new perspective. Dr. Allan L. Reiss of Stanford University in California says, "We seem to be rewarded by humor." Humor can act as a "third person" enabling a person to see his situation in terms of "the big picture". Humor helps us see when our fears are exaggerated or simply creating more stress and frustration.

Thus, the power of humor is its ability to stimulate change and shift perspectives — for instance: two elderly men are out walking their dogs. They came upon a coffee shop and decided to drop in, but the shop does not allow dogs. Aha! They think; we'll pretend our dogs are Seeing Eye dogs. The first man goes in with his German Shepherd judiciously bumping into the counter, and he's not challenged. So, the second man goes in mimicking his friend. The owner says, "You can't bring that dog in here!" "But, this is a Seeing Eye dog." The fellow explains. "A Chihuahua can't be a seeing eye dog!" the owner retorts. "A Chihuahua!" exclaims the quick-witted dog walker. "You mean they gave me a Chihuahua?" Perspective is everything — humor can give you the power to control perspective.

One day, while making my rounds through the children's ward in a local hospital, I was asked to step into a room where a young boy lay suffering from depression and withdrawal. He hadn't uttered a word for three days. The parents had asked me to visit the child as they had seen me at a circus performance earlier. I sat next to the boy for some time. In a soft voice, I began, "Ladies and gentlemen, boys and girls of all ages." His eyes opened. "Do you remember me from the circus?" A smile appeared on the boy's face. In a barely audible whisper he said, "You're Muggins the Clown." I sat talking with him about the circus. At the parents' request, I made it a point to visit the boy several times during his stay in the hospital. Each visit resulted in more conversation and his recovery eventually progressed to the point where he was able to leave the hospital. This story testifies to the power of humor in health and healing.

With all this research and testimonial evidence, you would think there would be a mad rush to accept humor as a serious contribution to health and healing. Wrong! There is considerable confusion and reluctance to empower ourselves through humor. Reluctance can result from not understanding that humor can make any mistake acceptable. The more we see life as a serious competitive environment in which we are judged as being good or evil, the less we are open to humor. Logically, then, how much humor an individual is willing to experience is actually a good test for the tolerance of emotional stress.

Our tendency to be suspicious of humor results from being taught in early childhood that a mature person must be a serious person. I can testify, though that some of the most dogmatically "serious" people I have met are confined in institutions! People with a sense of humor often see around problems. They usually are creative, open minded and — surprise — popular.

A sense of humor can signify emotional maturity, and some doctors believe the development of humor in their patients is an important indicator of whether they are well enough to leave the hospital.

A patient who displays a humorous attitude may be a patient who demonstrates the presence of a positive coping mechanism. *A patient asks his doctor, "What's wrong Doctor? You look puzzled." The Doctor says. "Well, I can't figure out what's is wrong with you. I think it's the result of heavy drinking." The patient responds, "Okay, I'll come back when you're sober."* Our perception of humor indicates progress.

The value of humor in healing is only beginning to be appreciated. Its usage is still a chance event and varies considerably from hospital to hospital. As an example: there are about 13 hospitals in my community. One of these uses a half dozen clowns, another only one, and the rest none. Most hospitals have no program using humor to improve health. There is generally no attempt at a planned use of humor by health professionals, although there is plenty of scientific evidence that humor and laughter are valuable for achieving good physical health and positive mental attitudes. Studies indicate that humor, when used constructively, can help communication by breaking down barriers, making people feel good and bringing people closer together. Humor can reassure, convey information and release tension.

You and I can use the power of humor to make a difference. Just like a friend of mine, Elizabeth, who was 70 pounds overweight after a lifetime roller-coaster ride through a variety of diet programs. They all involved diet and exercise; she always lost weight. And she always gained the weight back again sometimes more than she lost. Her worst problem, she told me, was night time when she becomes lonely, hungry and depressed.

One day she said, "Forrest, what am I going to do? I'm really disappointed in myself." I made her a two hour audiotape of jokes, printed a list of humor and laugh exercises and told her to use them every time she wanted to reach for food. To make a long story short, she lost the weight and I gained a friend. Trying to lose weight on diet and exercise is like milking a cow on a two legged stool; you're only going to fall off. It is the third leg of humor that makes all the difference.

When using humor there are some things to consider:

1. Accept humor as an integral part of your life. At first accepting humor may feel like rubbing a cat the wrong way; it feels strange. But this is because we are taught to be suspicious of humor. Develop your personal use of humor, use it sparingly at first — a little humor goes a long way. Teach yourself to see spontaneous opportunities for humor, which naturally evolves out of day-to-day experiences. (Comedy, on the other hand, is planned entertainment.) Be willing to risk using humor. Only those who risk going too far can know now far they can go.

2. Listen and learn about the "other" people because everyone sees humor differently. For example: a

woman goes to her doctor because her hearing is getting worse. The doctor said, "Mrs. Larson, your hearing isn't getting worse, you have a suppository in your ear." "Oh," said Mrs. Larson, "That explains what I did with my hearing aide." Now this story is not going to be humorous to everyone; in fact, it might well be offensive to some. It's important to know your listeners' level of humor and their ability to accept and deal with different kinds of humor. One way to reduce "risk" is to take the time to understand your listeners and how they respond to humor.

3   Be prepared to respond to other people's humor. Is your laugh sincere or forced? How do you let others know you are offended without causing a problem? Complimenting another's humor validates and supports them; it follows that you also can diminish their humor by silence or reacting with counter-humor. In the example of Mrs. Larson and her suppository you might make a face or say, "Uggh." Remember that leaving the person's jest dangling without a justified and responsible reply denies them the opportunity for growth.

"Be capable of taking yourself lightly and your work seriously" is more easily said than done. When my grandson makes "body sounds" at the dinner table, I want to jump out of my chair and stuff a napkin into his mouth. As tempting as that might be, I have to remind myself that I once behaved just as badly (some say worse). "Chill out Dad!" is my son's advice. Be willing to laugh at yourself and your failures. Doing so opens up the opportunity to accept new ideas and change without loss of self-esteem.

Empowering your life through humor is a fantastic experience. In fact, you can get so enthusiastic you can drown your listeners in a flood of jokes and comedy. Each of us has a genuine and sincere sense of humor. When we copy humor from others, our own sense of humor becomes stilted, which makes us appear affected. Sit back and let your own sense of humor surface. A natural humor that comes from the heart is far better than an artificial humor that is perfect.

Having experienced the power of humor to improve our own health and well being, it is only natural to help others. STOP! The first question to resolve is, is this humor really for the sick person or for you? We are often frustrated and stressed out because a loved one is sick. Stress and frustration create tension. A good, self-motivated laugh might help deal with tension by distancing yourself temporarily from the situation. That's okay, but if your intention is to share humor with a sick friend or loved one to help them, make sure that's what you're doing. Some patients respond well to hospital jokes. One of my favorite is about *a man who bursts into the hospital room where his friend is laying ash white and limp in bed. "I have terrible news. The doctor said you have cancer and Alzheimer's disease." "Well", responded the patient, "At least I don't have cancer."* Sharing ridiculous stories can reduce tension. I like the one about *a bus driver in Zimbabwe, Africa transporting 20 mental patients. They had escaped while he stopped for a bathroom break. Not wanting to admit his incompetence, the driver went to a nearby bus stop and offered everyone waiting for a bus a free ride in his bus. He then delivered the passengers to the mental hospital, telling the staff that the patients were very excitable and prone to bizarre fantasies. The deception went undiscovered for three days.* The ridiculous events from daily life can reduce the suffering of others.

While you will learn that humor is a powerful tool, it is, after all, an individual experience. Two people might disagree as to what they find is funny. For instance: *"Doctor, there is an invisible man in your office!" The doctor responds, "Tell him I can't see him now."* To many people this little joke is not funny, but it makes me chuckle.

So, how do you find out what is (and what is not) funny? I have a little exercise that might help. Describe three people you feel have a great sense of humor. Write down the characteristics or behavior they have that you find amusing. The common characteristics in these people are what you see as humorous. Now that you have identified these characteristics you can share your observations with others and find out what makes their funny bones work. In this way you can grow and strengthen your humor skills.

Humor is like perfume. You can't share it with others without getting it on yourself. Humor is both infectious and contagious. The infectious and contagious elements of humor help you help others to heal.

Many of us are naturally inclined to be suspicious of jokes. "Doctor I feel terrible. I feel like a pair of curtains." Doctor responds, "Now, now, pull yourself together." Oh, that was a horrible joke! Let's face it, not everyone has the predisposition or the communication skills for generating or receiving comedy. But remember, comedy is entertainment; humor comes from within. It is both spontaneous and natural.

Still, many people cannot (or will not) use humor to improve their health or to heal themselves. This is understandable. When a person is ill, the reality of his illness can tend to make him withdraw, become depressed and reject humorous messages. "Go away and leave me alone!" is his response to proffered help. Sometimes we just need to be alone to "enjoy" our ill health.

Some people suffer more from exaggeration and fear than from the actual illness. "Doctor, I don't know what is wrong with me. I hurt all over. It hurts when I touch my shoulder. It hurts when I touch my foot. It hurts when I touch my stomach. It hurts when I touch my head." The doctor says, "I believe you've broken your finger."

The "I've got good news and bad news" routine is an approach that helps those who are too ill to ease their perhaps exaggerated responses to illness. For example: Golf courses in heaven are fantastically beautiful and always free. The bad news is that you have a tee off time in two hours.

Another light-hearted approach to patients is "The Other Patient" where you tell them about a person with similar concerns and — Guess what? — they had a great recovery! But be careful with this. True humor develops from the situation. Think of the Candy Striper who takes a trolley of goodies from one hospital room to the other. She stops in and says to a patient, "Would you like a cup of coffee?" "No," the patient responds, "I can't sleep when I drink coffee." "I have a similar problem," said the Candy Striper, "I can't drink coffee when I sleep."

Humor can help us see the "big picture". A patient complains to the doctor that his feet continually hurt. After careful examination, the doctor tells the patient to stop biting his nails. Or; A man gets up every morning with a headache until his wife tells him to get out of bed feet first.

People in hospitals find themselves in an unfamiliar environment among strangers and sometimes afraid. You can help by making regular calls; sharing humor from the local newspaper and community events. Whatever the situation, the purpose of using humor for others is to help make their burdens more bearable.

Humor Is an Important Aide
in Weight Control

Weight control is a serious issue in the Twenty-First Century. Any person attempting to artificially control their weight through diet and exercise should do so with the assistance of professionals. Humor plays an important role in controlling diet. In the beginning humor can change our perspective of weight from a stress filled reality to keeping the weight off when you have reached your objective.

Stress could be a contributor to obesity. Anger, guilt, remorse and regret are stress contributors that can be anesthetized by the consumption of food. We cannot change the past, but we can change our perspective by substituting humorous experiences for food. We can be with friends in a non-food environment. A telephone call, a letter, going to a movie (don't eat the popcorn) or going to a live program in exchange for eating snacks at home alone is a good place to start. *Follow your doctors advice!* Buy some taped comedy or upbeat music to play while you are exercising. If you are walking, give a cheerful "hello" to people passing by. So what if they do not respond, the purpose is to reinforce your cheerful attitude. Try not to eat your meals while watching television. Television can condition you to feel hungry when it is combined with food. Try to stay away from food commercials. This is difficult as food commercials usually come on right at dinner time. But, you can schedule your meals to avoid these times. You can put your control on "mute" to reduce stimulus. You can also reward yourself (not with calories) for getting through food commercials without even a snack.

I have had a weight problem for years. My worst time is at night. I really am not hungry, but my stomach screams for food. Especially for the food I should not have. I have tried rules such as "No carbs after 6 p.m.;" none of them work. What does work best is a combination of short exercise with my mind filled with humor. I do sit-ups and curl-ups for about half an hour. During this time I recall all the stupid things that have happened to either me or others. I remember that stupid date I had. I remember funny things from my childhood. I like to pick a year from the past and think of three funny events from that year. When finished, I am tired and certainly not hungry. Try it, and see if this doesn't work for you.

Keeping the weight off is where most of us fail. There are many reasons. The most common reason is that we go back to eating the wrong things and again see life as serious and competitive. This is the time to take humor seriously. Sustain the humor you have developed. Expand upon your humor by focusing on the humor in the newspaper and magazines. Avoid loneliness by creating ways to get away and see the humor in creation, friends or watching people in public places. I keep a joke book by my bed. If I wake up and feel hungry, I feed on jokes (not food). TV is an important part of our lives, but make sure it contributes to your health and humor.

Humor in the Professional Health Care System

Health care practitioners often spend years training for their professions. Doctors have their coats, nurses have their caps and (where they still exist) Candy Stripers have their red and white striped outfits. There's a serious stratification with a built-in elitism in almost every healthcare institution. A by-product of this reality is a common worry that the use of humor might compromise the reputation of a professional health provider.

Yet humor is very much a part of the health care system. An ophthalmologist is conducting an eye exam with the patient 20 feet away from the eye chart. The doctor had the patient cover first his left eye, then his right while reading the chart. In both cases the patient could read perfectly right up to the 20/20 line. Then the doctor said, "Now both." Followed by silence — the patient was covering up both eyes!

• •

Humor evolves from real events. The professional caregiver can find these events an easy entry point to access and share humor. Professional caregivers can still maintain professionalism while adopting a lighter style of interaction with both patients and staff.

WARNING! If you are new to the health care environment, establish your competence first (especially among other staff members) and then let your sense of humor emerge. Patients usually welcome a lighter style of interaction.

Health care systems have found that patients do not interpret humor as indifference about their condition. This is particularly true when the caregiver's style of humor is respectful. It helps if you are sensitive to the patient's response to your humor. So, don't force your humor upon the patient. Think of humor as a medication. You must administer the right medicine, in the right dosage at the right time, in order to achieve the greatest benefits.

Remember, patients with similar symptoms do not always require the same medicine, and a similar rule applies to humor. Sometimes patients just don't feel like laughing. They may be nauseated, in pain or just not in the mood. When in doubt, smile rather than laugh. In other cases, patients may not be emotionally ready to respond to humor until they have come to accept the reality of their health problem. Don't try to use humor to subdue their depression or anger; wait and be a friendly companion. The time may come, however, when humor can help them turn the corner of acceptance or align their will to overcoming their illness.

Hospital staffs too generally use the same coping mechanisms that we all use when facing stressful situations. People get angry, depressed, withdrawn, anxious, assertive or demanding as they try to cope with stress. Once you know the patient or staff person well enough, you'll find that there is a corresponding style of humor for dealing with each of these coping mechanisms. It is good to be sensitive to how others are responding to your playful style.

One day a doctor told a woman that her husband had died of a massive heart attack. The medical term he used was "myocardial infarct". A few minutes later he overheard the woman on the phone tell family members that he had died of a "massive internal fart." Humor evolves from acceptable mistakes that happen during our daily experiences. How we use this humor in the professional workplace is a different matter.

Using humor is inappropriate when the patient:

• Needs time to cry

• Needs quiet time to rest, contemplate or pray

• Is trying to come to grips with any emotional crisis

• Is trying to communicate something important to you, or

• Someone in an adjacent bed is very sick or dying

Always avoid humor that is:

• Ethnic, sarcastic or mocking

• At the expense of another person (Laugh with someone not at them)

• Joking about any patient or their medical condition

Miscommunication creates most of the humor we experience. A patient came to his doctor for a routine checkup. He informed the doctor that he was having trouble with one of his medications. "Which one?" asked the Doctor? "The Patch." was the reply. "The nurse told me to put one on every six hours and now I'm running out of places on my body to put them." Examination revealed that the patient was not removing the old patch before applying new ones! Since humor is any acceptable mistake, the staff saw this mistaken communication as humorous. The patient might not see the humor at this time in his life. It may be unrealistic to expect patients to react favorably to humor when their health is threatened or they are embarrassed.

Clowning Around in Healing Institutions:

There are estimated to be about 8,000 clowns scattered around the United States. These clowns share a mysterious and almost unbelievable experience — that of a caterpillar emerging from its chrysalis as a beautiful butterfly.

All clowns have a life outside of clowning. Yet for some reason, putting on clown face and costume releases inhibitions and enables a whole new personality to emerge. The "everyday person" who inhabits Cha-Cha (a "South of the Border" clown) is a very conservative person. That is, until she gets into her clown face and costume! Suddenly she emerges as a vivacious Caribbean dance girl. This aspect of being a clown is a real joy. The public accepts a clown doing things as a clown that might otherwise be considered "weird". This "freedom" supported by the community opens up many avenues for fun and play. Many senior citizens become volunteer clowns in hospitals and other care facilities because of the rewards of bringing joy and happiness to others.

From this perspective many people consider the ultimate involvement of humor in terms of health and healing, is to become a "Caring Clown." Caring Clowns work as volunteers in hospitals and care facilities around the world. To become a Caring Clown, you first need to "find the clown" that is inside you and to develop your skills as a clown. You need not be alone in this process. The easiest way to become a clown is to connect to an experienced clown or clown club (called an "alley") in your local community. You will develop your clown name, costume and physical characteristics as you watch and work with more experienced clowns. Armed with these simple characteristics, you too can experience the wonderful power of humor to help people heal.

Of course, common sense needs to be applied. You do not want to frighten people. Patients who are very young or ill may be easily intimidated by garish and contradictory colors. The worse thing you can do is to smear a bunch of lipstick on your face, put on some flamingo pink wig and parade around in a purple and green striped pajama styled costume. In fact, the first thing Caring Clowns do is to make sure that their costumes are not frightening. Include cool colors. I particularly like to emphasize the soothing color blue. Blend your facial colors, to eliminate grotesque features and leave only those accents that identify your character.

If you use a costume that identifies you as a caricature of a doctor or other hospital staff member, keep those identifying features to a minimum. Remember, many patients fear hospital staff as they can represent pain, bad news or more stress.

The next thing to do is to call the volunteer services department of your local hospital. They will send you information regarding their facility's guidelines for Caring Clown volunteers. Read over the material and ask questions before you volunteer. Different hospitals have different regulations and expectations; some provide minimal levels of compensation and some do not.

Caring Clowns are different from other clowns in that they focus on listening rather than performing. Short tricks and simple games work, but elaborate routines don't fit the setting. I carry pads of notepaper, a pocket full of pencils, a finger puppet, a small bottle of bubble solution and some stickers. I also include "hand wipes" in order to sanitize the pencils after a visit. My games are usually tick-tack-toe ("naughts and crosses" to the British) and hangman. However, I use conversation as my principle tool during a visit. Sometimes, my silence and compassionate listening are the most important element of my conversations with both hospital patients and staff.

As a Caring Clown, I want to connect to the patient, the institutional staff members or the family and friends of the patient. I need to be there for them in the hospital room, the waiting room, the cafeteria, the hallway or the chapel. One minute I may be laughing boisterously and the next silently holding the hand of a dying child. I am not there to be a comic or to be silly. I am there to fulfill whatever they need from me. Sometimes I'll do magic tricks for a whole swarm of kids and then move to listen to an old man in a single room tell about his experiences during World War II. The challenge as a Caring Clown is that I must be spontaneous. I want to be aware of the ever-changing environment of the institution. I may even keep notes so that I can sit in staff meetings and contribute worthwhile information. To be humorous is also to take humor seriously.

I see my behavior as sensitive, yet playful. "Play" activity can include helping a patient prepare mentally and emotionally for an operation or for procedures that may be threatening or painful. Play can be directed to help the patient's family or the hospital staff, so that they can more easily express themselves. Play can be effective as a diversion; many people in hospitals are coping with serious illnesses that rob them of the normal pleasures of life. Patients, relatives and staff may be dealing with life and death issues at any given moment. Play gives them some space to relax, forget for a moment and maybe even laugh. Remember, laughter is good for the immune system!

One of the greatest benefits of this work is that the Caring Clown fits in where other staff members do not. The clown has the time to be extra gentle, to play and to have fun. The clown's presence creates a sense of trust that allows patients to share their thoughts and feelings. The clown is in a unique position to listen. In the swirling, bustling activity of most institutions, there is little time for this precious activity.

Most care-giving institutions focus on the physical body. The mere presence of a clown, by contrast, is a merry predicament that invites a smile and gives staff, patients and visitors permission to play. Clowns bring fantasy, theater and compassion into the hospital room.

I always keep in mind that the patients' rooms are their homes, their lavatories, prayer spaces, and their only place for privacy. It is imperative that I gain their permission before entering their room. There are many ways to get permission. I usually schedule my appearance through the head nurse or other institutional officials, so that the patient has the joy of anticipation. In addition, it is always advisable to obtain any medical, or other pertinent information that is allowable before entering the room. In short, "be prepared."

I always know the names of those in the room. If I pass a room with the door open, and I am informed that the person might like my visit, I always get permission before entering. I use my finger puppet. I extend my arm with the puppet on my finger in the room. Wiggling my finger, the puppet asks if they would like a visit. If not, I show my appreciation and go on my way.

Sanitation is always a concern in health care institutions. Your must participate in training that will help make you aware of how to deal with cleanliness. Clowns must be especially cautious about contamination. Sit in chairs or stand rather than sit on the bed. Sanitize your hands and ALL play materials after leaving any room.

One of the major differences between clowning in general and clowning in hospitals is that hospitals are serious, health care institutions with complex rules. Clowns must present themselves as a gentle presence, respecting the boundaries and rules, yet bringing a very special healing energy to those in need.

Not surprisingly, some care facilities are reluctant to accept clowns. Hospitals see clowns only as entertainment. Yet, slowly, many hospitals are beginning to see clowns as part of their staff. The primary concern for hospitals, of course, is to provide safe care for their patients. Federal and State agencies conduct inspections to ensure they do so, and do not pose any unnecessary risks for patients or staff. Now imagine a clown merrily trudging through their hallways, popping into wards and private rooms looking like something that escaped from a bad horror movie. Envision patients screaming and pulling out their IV's, bedpans sliding across the floor as the patients panic. Can you see why hospitals might hesitate to have a clown on staff? Don't take it personally if you call a hospital and they decline your services as a Caring Clown. Down the road there will be another health provider willing to cooperate.

The general public sees clowns as circus, party and stage entertainers. But why aren't clowns invited into the boardrooms of corporate America? At issue is the question of integrity and trust. Street entertainers and clowns are perceived as poorly educated, politically naive and socially inept. It is going to be a slow process, but caring clowns must build and maintain trust. This will be accomplished through learning and following hospital protocols, complying with doctor's orders, being professionally competent and honoring the patient's rights and boundaries. This educational process can not take place without the cooperation and support of the hospital.

So, let's say you've passed the hospital volunteer program requirements and are now a certified Caring Clown. The most important thing you have to offer patients and their families is yourself. Here's a helpful list of some items you should not bring into a hospital:

• Pets or animals that are prohibited

• Balloons (most hospitals want to be latex free)

• Large props (hospital rooms are crowded with furniture, equipment and people)

When people are really, really sick; they want to be alone. Sleep is a precious commodity, especially amid the clamor of a hospital. Sitting up in bed may make some patients dizzy or nauseous. As a Caring Clown we must learn to avoid sensitive areas in the hospital such as intensive care, emotionally ill patients, those undergoing surgery or serious procedures and those who need protective isolation. The best way to stay out of trouble is always to go through the nursing stations. While you're there, the staff could use a little humor! Once in a long while, I have even known doctors who put on a red clown nose to show support for caring clowns.

Being a successful Caring Clown is really easy. Below are four things to consider. Heeding these four simple suggestions will make you a welcome clown in any hospital or care institution:

• Listen to the patients and encourage them to share their thoughts and feelings. Older patients as well as the very young particularly need someone who will take the time to listen to them.

• Empathize with their feelings. A gentle smile, a thoughtful comment, interest in their pets, school, hobbies or past experiences can make all the difference to patients.

• Stay in your clown character. Sometimes it is easy to lose yourself in the life of the patient, but remember you've put a lot of time and creative energy developing the character behind the costume and face. Staying in character allows the patient more freedom to respond in ways that will meet her needs.

• Notify a professional about any observation or patients' request that concerns you. When in doubt, report to staff or clergy.

What I like about being a Caring Clown are all the various activities and skills available to develop and share with the patients. Magic, puppets, games, and face painting — you name it! They all bring their own kind of fun. Face painting is very popular because the art work is so much appreciated. Some guidelines for face painting on hospital patients include:

• Never paint an area that has open wounds, rashes, severe acne or any surgical incision.

• Wipe the face with a pre-moistened, disposable towelette.

• Only use paint designated for face painting.

• Do not use metallic glitter.

• Use water-soluble paint that comes in tubes.

• Use a clean palette for each patient when mixing your colors.

• Use disposable makeup applicators to apply the paint.

At the end of your day, wash all your supplies in hot water with a soap that contains an antimicrobial agent.

Being a caring clown brings you into contact with the frail, the sick and the handicapped. Those who work as Caring Clowns invariably agree that they receive far more than they give. When you use humor to help others, you make connections with individuals who accept you into their lives during very vulnerable moments. Helping them can enhance your sense of perspective on life, help maintain your sense of humor and give you a sense of well-being. For me, as well as many others, caring means the sharing of humor.

Forrest "Muggins" Wheeler entertains
children at a local hospital.

Chapter Five

Humor and Gender

"I can never tell when you're serious."

Chapter 5 deals with how humor is viewed differently by women than by men. It shows how each gender uses humor and comedy for different purposes.

Chapter 5 enables you to apply this knowledge in situations where men and women are forced to relate to each other as in the workplace and the home.

Chapter Five

Humor and Gender

How to please a woman?
Love her, take her to dinner, miss the
"Superbowl" for her, buy her jewelry, act inter-
ested in what she has to say...
How to please a Man?
Show up naked, bring beer.

— Unknown

A man and his wife are attending a party. The husband starts flirting with one of the women. A man says to the wife, "Doesn't it bother you to see your husband making passes at another woman?" "Well no, not really" was the reply. "Just because a dog chases cars doesn't mean he knows how to drive".

Perception, communication and misunderstanding between the genders have been the source of humor for centuries. Nowhere is this more apparent than in the distribution of household responsibilities, negotiation is the rule. For example, in my household, there was a debate over who should make the coffee every morning. My wife said, "You, my dearest and loving husband, should, because you get up first, and then we don't have to wait as long to get our coffee." But my response was, "You are in charge of the kitchen and cooking around here, and you should do it, because it is your job. I can wait for my coffee." To this, my wife retorts, "No, you should do it, and besides, it is in the Bible that the man should make the coffee." Completely baffled, my defense was, "I can't believe that, show me." So, she fetched the Bible, opens it up to the New Testament and there at the top of the page, was printed: "HEBREWS."

It does not take a rocket scientist to see that there is a decided difference in how men and women see and use humor. Much of this perception revolves around the use of power, logic and territory. Take for example the story of who should make the coffee. The husband's position is one of territory. His wife is in charge of the kitchen and he should stay out. Conversely, her position is one of convenience. To her, it only makes sense that the first to rise should make the coffee. Thus, the interpretation of the male tends to reflect the use of territory, whereas the wife is dealing with the logic of what is most convenient. The contradiction of perspective creates an opportunity for tension. The wife, seeing the danger, uses humor to deflect the tension.

Although men and women view the same situation differently, these differences change over the years. Fifty years ago, much of the humor centered on the wife at home, the husband at work and their relationship with their children and family members. Today, much of our humor is about issues such as divorce, women in the work force, individual rights and sexual freedom. Much of this humor is based upon absurd generalizations. For instance, *"What is the difference between men and government bonds?" Answer: "Government bonds mature."* Being conscious of the ever changing shifts of social issues helps us use humor to make friends, distance ourselves from unpleasant situations and increase productivity when coming into contact with the opposite sex..

A man is sitting at a bar talking to a very beautiful woman. She leans over and whispers in his ear, "Make me feel like a real woman." So, the man takes off his jacket. Hands it to her and says, "Here, iron this." While this joke might have been accepted around the 1920s, today many women might be offended. What is the difference? Eighty years ago women were taught to be mothers and caregivers. Today women pride themselves on equality with men. Today, some women see this joke as spoof on men and how bungling and sexist they are perceived to be. Gender roles and the humor that goes along with these roles have changed.

When we know how humor and gender have changed in relation to each other we are better able to predict what is ahead and avoid the mistakes of the past. About 150 years ago most of us lived on farms. The men worked in the field and the women worked in the home. Education was only important to instill the ability to read, write and do math. It was an agriculturally-based society. The sexes exhibited a "separate, but equal" sharing of both power and humor. Men's humor tended to center on issues and activities outside of the home. There's a humorous story from this time period that goes like this: *A farmer put an ad in the paper that said, "Need wife who owns her own horse. Please send picture of the horse."* Wives had to be strong, good workers, religious and very healthy.

On the other hand, women's humor tended to involve relationship-oriented activities and issues within the home. There was a sign in a farmhouse kitchen on which these words were printed: "Honesty is the best policy, but sometimes, keeping your mouth shut is even better." Remnants of this past are still evident today in rural America. We see this at county fairs where women compete in domestic skills such as cooking, while men compete in rodeo contests. We see this in city and suburban church organizations where there are clubs that support women's quilting groups and the men guide sports teams and camping activities. Being aware of these differences empowers you to adjust your humor to the situation in which you find yourself.

When you travel around this planet, you will find many societies that connect power and territory giving power to the males (patriarchal). In other societies, the power base rests firmly with the female (matriarchal). Matriarchal and patriarchal powers are different. With men the common image is of a cave man dragging a female home to his cave. Power in this paradigm means ownership of property, often with physical boundaries. Female power most often has to do with the handling of money, and decision making over marriages, funerals and cultural dominance.

Images and myths of power are different between the genders. The male image is muscular, the female image is beauty. These types of images, along with jokes and humor illustrating the shifts between male and female control, are common throughout history and in all societies. The reality is that power is constantly in negotiation and flux between individuals. Examples of humor based around the so-called "war between the sexes" are practically endless. A man says to his wife, "Let's change jobs." The wife says, "Fine by me. You get the children fed and dressed and I'll go out and honk the horn for ten minutes."

Laughter and humor can neutralize hard feelings around power struggles. While culturally, power may rest with a specific gender, laughter and humor can change the base of power depending upon individual situations and relationships. "My wife lets me make all the important decisions. But, she gets to decide which decisions are important."

Humor can eliminate territorial struggles through negotiation. One such territory is the kitchen. Who does the cooking and who does the cleaning is often open to negotiation. Jane and Mary were discussing marriage. Jane said, "My husband and I have been married for five years and every night he complains about the food. Mary asked, "Gosh, doesn't that just irritate you? Jane responded, "No, not as long as he does the cooking."

The Evolution of Gender Based Humor

As population increased and available land decreased people moved to the city where there was work. Modern technology created employment and cheap products. In 1929 came the Great Depression. Many women had to join their husbands and work outside the home in order to feed, clothe and provide shelter for their families. Humor moved from farm experiences and problems to city and factory.

World War II encouraged women to take on roles previously reserved for men. When the men left to serve their country in the military, women became machinists, truck drivers and "bosses." Women proved they were just as competent in these roles as men were. For the first time in history, thousands of women both earned and spent money independent of men. Salaried women began to perceive their married roles differently than those women who entered marriage without work experience. Some men were threatened by this change. As one man put it, "I believe women should stick to the shopping for food, cleaning, ironing, cooking, washing dishes and taking care of the kids. No wife of mine is going to work." Women, who were financially independent because they worked, saw marriage more as a co-opted relationship of strengths and weaknesses and expected men to participate more fully in domestic duties. Women who entered marriage having no work experience, not expecting to work outside the home, saw their role as supportive and "traditional." During this time, it became more common to experience attitudes of equality, as well as the sharing of sexually explicit humor between genders.

Before 1945, men often postponed marriage until they were financially able to support a wife and family. In spite of the new conception of women with the proud biceps of "Rosie the Riveter" and the sense of self-sufficiency and ability they had demonstrated, traditionally, the man was once again supposed to "wear the pants" in the family. However, the purchasing power of two working adults became very attractive, especially as post-war advertisements shifted their messages from having things we need to needing things we want. A man went into a store and applied for credit. "Do you have any references, asked the store manager?" "Sure," was the reply, "I owe every store in town." The desire to "keep up with the Jones further stressed marital relationships as earning and spending became another power issue between the genders. "You have to give my wife a lot of credit. She can't get along without it." As traditional gender roles became more subtle and complex, there were no real role models. People were entering new territory. More and more marriages buckled under the pressure and ended in divorce. The changing viewpoint in society towards seeing marriage as a knot tied by a minister and untied by a lawyer is illustrated in the joke about a woman who said to her divorce attorney, "My husband always said that everything he has is mine. Well, now I want it."

A minister got married and he and his wife had a beautiful daughter. A year later they had a handsome little boy. A year later they had twins. Deciding they had enough children they went to family planning. During consultation, the minister explained that God had truly blessed them and if His will was for them to have lots of children, then they would somehow manage. The counselor the couple went to said, "Yes, but God also gave you a brain and the capacity to limit the number of your children."

With the introduction of the birth control pill in the sixties, women no longer had to fear pregnancy. This changed the way women and men socialized. Women were now able to take control of their sex lives. For the first time, women were free to have just as much fun as their male counterparts. *"Are you familiar with Judy Brown?" Response: "I tried to be, but she belted me."* This joke from the sixties illustrates men's amazement as women became less passive in terms of who had the sexual power and how this power is managed. In spite of, or perhaps because of all the new options, divorce rates continued to escalate and the "single mom" became increasingly common.

As women reevaluated their role as homemaker and caregiver, men had to reassess their own roles and base of authority. One man said to another, *"I finally figured out why they call it the mother tongue. Father never gets a chance to use it."* Many men became fearful of marriage, and began to see it as a "trap." The following, male-oriented joke demonstrates this: *A man placed an advertisement in the classifieds stating, "Wife Wanted." He soon received 100 letters. They all said the same thing, "You can have mine."*

The male perspective was different from women's. Men began to fear that some women would use marriage strictly as an opportunity for financial gain through divorce and alimony. Men could not tell the difference between women who wanted a permanent relationship based upon the desire for family and women who saw marriage as an opportunity to become monetarily secure — and independent. They saw other men become financially ruined and psychologically destroyed through divorce, and their humor began to reflect their fears: *"I never knew what real happiness was until I got married; and then it was too late."*

Men began to see women's humor as reflecting open hostility towards men. *Question: "What would you do if you saw your cheating husband rolling around in pain on the*

· ·

ground?" Answer: "Shoot him again." Women became less dependent upon men, and in many cases resentful. *Question: "How many men does it take to screw in a light bulb?" Answer: "One — he just holds it and waits for the world to revolve around him."* Men's humor became just as hostile, *"How many feminists does it take to change a light bulb?" Answer: "One to change the light bulb and fifteen to form a support group."*

Women have become keenly aware of social and financial inequality and find it very unacceptable. Men receive more money than women do for performing the same job. Men receive promotions over more competent and skilled women. Language (both oral and written) often favors men at the expense of women. Access to credit is easier for men than it is for women. Medical research favors men while not serving the needs and issues of women. Fringe benefits to meet women's needs in pregnancy are negligible in the corporate environment. A sign on the desk of a modern woman, working in the corporate environment, demonstrates a humorous, female response to this kind of inequality: *"Of course I don't look as busy as the men ... I did it right the first time."*

As women have organized to meet these concerns, gender roles have been challenged further. As one man put it, "I am sure glad my wife joined the women's concerns group. Now she complains about all men and not just about me." Some women have found previously acceptable male behavior as demeaning. They don't want men opening car doors for them. They want the same status as men when it comes to paying for dinner and entertainment. Women drive trucks, operate forklifts and perform other manual labor previously reserved for men. Women's presence in the professions of law, medicine and executive management has become more and more evident.

All these changes created a new kind of humor: "Can you imagine a world without men? No crime and lots of happy, overweight women." Sadly, men and women have become increasingly hostile and suspicious of each other. The humor we hear today reflects this: "When all is said and done, men still have the last word; it's, 'Yes, dear.'"

In modern electronic societies, women and men apparently are becoming less dependent upon each other. In general, the end of the Twentieth Century saw some men and women going in separate directions. The changes in our humor reflect this. "Sometimes I wish my wife were my mother. Then I could run away from home." Along with the gender clash, other dynamics of contemporary society have drastically shifted humans from traditional roles and associations of extended family. The elderly feel less responsible for their children. A bumper sticker on an expensive motor home reads, "We're joyfully spending our children's inheritance."

There have always been negotiations of power between the genders based on family wealth and background, psychological dominance, relationships with other family members or education. Humor can play an important role in the continuing process of successful adjustments and negotiations between genders. That's why understanding the differences in humor, as defined by gender, is so useful. Possession of this knowledge can help you diffuse hard feelings, resolve power struggles and grease the gears of social interaction. Given the built in difficulties between genders in our modern society, we need all the help we can muster in order to relate to each other in a manner that serves everyone. If you allow it, humor can come to your rescue.

How Are They Different?

We've already seen how, while both men and women use humor, their approach to it is from different points of

• •

view. Where men tell jokes, women tell humorous stories. The following joke is generally loved by men and disliked by women: *An office manager says; "Women are all the same. I got a secretary at the office who is getting a little behind in her work, and a wife who's getting a big behind at home."* Women object to the element of ridicule. In contrast, women prefer jokes involving situations. *Two women are talking and one says to the other, "Men think all we want is their money. All I want is a husband who is good looking, kind and sensitive. I don't think that is too much to ask of a millionaire, do you?"* Women like this kind of humor because it promotes conversation.

If you noticed an element of conflict between the genders, this is to be expected. It is because men and women see the same situation from different points of view. Humor can ease the tension and allow room for new ideas. Satirical barbs directed at the other gender bring the conflict out in the open. *"Why do men give their most intimate body part a name?" Answer, "Because they can't stand the thought of a stranger making 90 percent of their decisions for them."* This calls for a vote of approval or disapproval and opens the possibility of discussing some concerns.

What's Funny to Guys?

A joke is a short self-contained bit of humor that asserts a message, used to establish dominance or to seek social approval. Humorous stories are similar to jokes except they are continuous and tend to create conversation. Men tend to like jokes because they are efficient, practical and contain rules. "Did you hear the one" — immediately announces that a joke is going to be told. You are expected to laugh. If you do not, the teller of the joke will perceive social disapproval. Male humor often centers on politics, economics and sports and family because these are considered "male". In typically male-oriented humor, *an office worker is asked, "Who are you working for these days?" His answer reflects the age-old, male resignation to the power struggle between genders, "The same old outfit; my wife and our six kids."*

Men enjoy physical, adolescent and sexual-stereotype humor. Men often use humor to deal with tension created in a competitive market with limited resources. *"Women keep saying they want to get a man's salary. My wife does."* Sometimes men tell jokes to be competitive and aggressive, starting out by announcing they are going to tell you a joke — and you are going to listen. When done, you are *expected* to laugh. This might be followed by someone else telling another joke. The result is a game of "Can You Top This?" In dealing with stress caused by the need to make money and control over how it is spent, a man might express humor by saying, *"I'm losing the war on poverty because my wife fraternizes with the enemy."* This type of humor illustrates that men feel a lack of control over family finances.

Dad is paying the bills. He looks up and says to his wife, "You are spending us into the poorhouse." This is a comment that can easily engage both parties in confrontation, which will end in a power struggle where everyone loses. Rather than rising to the bait, his wife could respond with her own humor, saying, "You know dear, the poorhouse might provide us with more room." This satirical response is the kind of humor men can appreciate. It acknowledges concern, yet communicates confidence in money management and diffuses a potentially confrontational dynamic. In many situations, it can be more effective to meet the male's expression of his fears with humor, making light of the situation, rather than counter-attacking.

What's Funny to Gals?

Women's comedy is more prone to self-criticism than competition. Women are less likely to engage in practical jokes and pranks. The basic function of women's humor is to maintain connections with people. Women's humor tends to be more conversational, centering on relationships. A woman was being pestered by an admiring friend. When the friend called at two in the afternoon, she replied, "I do not accept calls after twelve noon. So the admirer called at eleven the next morning. "I do not accept calls before noon she stated with a crisp tone to her voice. To this the admirer pleaded, "I'll never be able to talk to you on the phone." To this the girl melodically responded, "Nice, isn't it." Women's humor also tends to be more anecdotal, involving wordplay based upon their own experiences or experiences of their friends and family: *"I had a relationship that lasted 13 years and ended just like that. I suggested that we stay friends. He said, 'OK, Mom.'"*

For women, humor functions more as a means of communication than as a means of self-presentation or cleverness. The goal of women's humor is interaction and intimacy, which tends to support others by demonstrating what they have in common. Women's humor also addresses problems with "double-duty" (housekeeping and outside careers). Women's humor reflects both connectedness and resistance, in terms of attacking the stereotypes that have restricted women.

Women rarely make fun of what people cannot change, such as social handicaps (stuttering) or physical appearances. However, women's humor will attack the deliberate choices that people make, which reveal hypocrisies, affectations, the mindless following of social expectations, and so on. Women laugh at the boss *"I have to admire my boss, if I don't I might get fired."* They laugh at social institutions. "I have to go to my church really early if I want to get a seat in the back row." Women laugh at situations. "It takes a lot of willpower, but I've finally given up trying to lose weight." Through laughter, women take social oppression and turn it around to create something new.

Women tend to use humor to share stories drawn from their lives, the problems of relationships, child rearing and career climbing. Women's humor is more participatory. "Oh, when I was a young girl, I wanted to have my hair like Jan Brady." And someone else will respond, "Oh, and those bell bottoms." Everybody is adding words and phrases and everybody is laughing, and gets a chance to have a turn. "Yesterday I was driving home and I reached into my purse for a lip balm, which I put on, you know, thoughtlessly like you do. I stopped for gas, got out to use the restroom and noticed how everyone was smiling at me. I thought, I'm really looking good today. When I went into the bathroom, I saw what everyone was smiling at; instead of clear lip balm, I had smeared red lipstick all over my mouth — like a clown." Everyone laughs and then shares their experiences with embarrassing situations. Men listening to this conversation might think, "Where's the humor? I don't get it." That's because men tend not to tell jokes at their own expense. Men tend to tell jokes at somebody else's expense. This phenomenon is neither good nor bad. It simply illustrates the gender differences in how humor is generated and experienced.

In the last few decades, the sexes have identified their differences and used humor to seek compromise, understanding and resolution. Humor between and among the sexes can be used to:

1. Build cohesiveness in a group and serve as a social lubricant. More social equality and freedom to intermingle has tended to blur the distinction between gender-based humor. Men and women

associate with each other in a rich variety of scenarios, making the sharing of humor reflecting shared interests and concerns more common and acceptable.

2. Entertain, either to wake a group up, or to serve as a tool to educate. Humor can serve to bring to our attention imbalances in our society or behavior. Entertainment can offer a safer risk-free avenue of communication. When addressing a particular issue, start by being willing to listen to those involved, regardless of gender. Using wit and humor to inform others of your viewpoints or concerns is a way to drive your viewpoints home in a memorable fashion. In this way, you can educate others while creating a safe environment for others to share their points of view.

3. Convincing people to achieve a specific purpose is a form of humor that can serve as a political, economic or social influence. Serious community problems such as drugs, domestic abuse and crime are commonly topics tackled within local organizations comprised of both genders. Although these topics are often rife with sensitivities about political, social and economic failures, humor can be quite effective in negotiating agendas. Being aware of how each gender processes information, (including humor) empowers you to be more effective in initiating change. Humor moves everyone's focus into the positive. By using humor to focus on possibilities, rather than impossibilities, you make yourself more effective while functioning within all manner of organizations.

Humor, Gender and the Work Place

There are two areas where the sexes tend to gather. One is around the home and family, the other is at work. Most of the subject of humor and gender has focused on home, family and social contact. With the growing issue of sexual harassment in the work environment, the role of humor needs particular attention.

The idea of work has centered on the attitude that if you had fun, or were joking, laughing or showing even a "playful attitude;" it was assumed that you were goofing off, unprofessional, immature or just not taking your work seriously enough. Work is where you go to get the resources for food, shelter and clothing. This is as serious as it gets. An inner office directive reflects this attitude. "Henceforth, there will be no laughter or smiling allowed in this building during working hours. Laughing distracts fellow employees. And, if you are smiling, you're not thinking about your work."

At the end of the Twentieth Century, however our two knights in shining armor (science technology and research) came to our rescue with data showing that when people start to have more fun at work they become energized and more productive and it provides an outlet for tension and stress. What is important is *to take your work seriously while taking yourself lightly* in doing your work. *Fortune* magazine's list of "The 100 Best Companies to Work for in America" were also the companies that placed a major emphasis on finding ways to help make work fun.

The question is: "What makes a job fun?" One obvious answer is to learn to find humor in our day-to-day experiences. Employees who believe that fun has positive effects tend to make work fun. Why not? Fun people are viewed as being intelligent, energetic, hardworking, outgoing, friendly, and competent, and possess a "sense of humor". These are precisely the qualities that many companies today seek when looking for new personnel.

To help you find your way to your own "fun persons" at work you may need to ask yourself, "Are you a reactive fun person, or a proactive fun person?" A reactive person tends to stand back, be non-competitive, supportive and pleasant to be around. A proactive person demonstrates a high level of energy, is intelligent, always there with constructive ideas, competitive and company motivated. It is this proactive person who can introduce elements of fun into your work place. Whether reactive, proactive or somewhere in between; there are things you can consider when putting "fun" into your work.

1. Humor Display. This can be a bulletin board or other display where anyone can add cartoons, poke fun at situations (be sure it is non-offensive). This humor display might facilitate communication between employees with needs and employees with resources. It is a good idea to change the board on a preplanned basis but keep the old material for future use.

2. Put some Humor in that "Break Room". Add cartoons, joke books, fun ideas, VCRs and audio receivers (include plenty of ear phones).

3. Insert stress relieving props. Have a stuffed item available to kick and maul, hula hoops or games for staff when they feel stressed out.

4. Have a dress-up day. Choose a theme or focus on a situation or holiday.

5. Provide awards for meeting quotas. Best posters and cartoons, toughest customer, and most humorous skit are some suggestions.

6. Photos of management "when they were children" on display.

7. Insert humor into your meetings.

8. Take a co-worker to coffee.

9. Hire future workers who are both competent and display a sense of humor.

10. Encourage top and middle management to exhibit humor.

Regardless of your choices and efforts, use good judgment and always take your work seriously and take yourself lightly.

Stress, Humor and the Work Place

Job stress continues to grow. It cost billions of dollars to deal with absenteeism, lost productivity and work related health problems that are stress related. Stress causes burnout, lowered motivation, cynicism, negative attitudes, frustration, feelings of rejection, loss of self-esteem and hopelessness. It lowers our ability to function and influences workers private lives as well. The United States is not the only country having these experiences. Japan had such high levels of stress from 1980 to 1999 that a new word was coined "karoshi." It described death due to overwork. Around 1995 job stress in England reached "epidemic proportions."

Increase in job stress is due to growing workloads, harder targets, performance related pay, fears about unemployment and hard driving management. Time off is one solution to this problem. Humor is another tool useful in dealing with stress. As your humor improves, you may find it easier to let go of office politics. Humor helps you deal with awkward situations. An employee was promoted, but now had to manage his co-workers. He dealt with this by saying, "Do not think of me as your boss. Think of me as a friend — a friend who is always right." Everyone laughed. Shared laughter helps soften an unpleasant reality. One manager walked into a meeting wearing a T-shirt with a bulls eye printed on it. "Okay," he said, "take your best shot."

We all make mistakes; humor takes away the concept of loss of pride or self esteem. Anything you can do to establish an atmosphere of "play" creates a non-judgment frame of mind. This is particularly true when dealing with differences of opinion. You need openness and comfort when working with difficult issues. Shared positive humor is a powerful way of achieving resolution without loss of prestige. Humor creates an atmosphere where opposing views are more likely to be expressed. It is like sticking your toe in water before jumping in. The reaction others have to your humor tells you if it's safe to proceed.

It is quite understandable if you are hesitant to inject humor into a sensitive situation. Here are some ideas that might help:

1. Before you start, be prepared.

2. It helps if your humor is connected to the point you need to make.

3. Make your point, illustrate it with humor, and then summarize your point.

4. Make fun of yourself, not someone else.

5. Refrain from offensive language, alcohol or smoking.

6. Keep in mind the effect of what you say if repeated out of context.

• •

As we move through the Twenty-First Century it is going to be harder to maintain a competitive edge. Those organizations that support innovative solutions to problems and create a work atmosphere which nurtures the creative skills of employees will have a higher survival rate than those who do not. Hal Rosenbluth, CEO of Rosenbluth International states; "We know that the only way for us to continuously provide solutions to the need of the ever-changing business world is to have the kind of environment where spontaneity thrives." Humor is essential in creating this kind of work place.

Today, we are inundated with constant and accelerating change. The growth of computers, video games, new developments in home entertainment and the Internet have reduced the opportunity for direct communication between the sexes and between individuals. These changes encourage life-styles unfettered by family history, neighborhood connections and societal pressures. In turn, we see this change in our use of humor. Story telling is becoming a lost art. Rather than creating and sharing our stories and humor with others, we feel comfortable turning our humor over to televised comedians who entertain us in the privacy and isolation of our homes. The daily sharing of humor with one another has also narrowed as we strive to be "politically correct," fearful of being perceived as insensitive to the special concerns and biases of others.

To sum things up, men and women have a long history of love/hate, nurture/violence. Novels both humorous and tragic testify to this everlasting struggle. Hopefully, this chapter has given you an opportunity to visualize yourself using humor as you deal with gender differences and conflict. In cross-gender relationships of work and play, humor creates needed space for communication. When things get tense, try using humor to change the subject or to cool down the situation. You do not have to be a jokester with a lampshade on your head to effect positive change in others or yourself. Find that "humor-bone" and nurture its growth. The rest will develop naturally — and humorously!"

Forest "Muggins" Wheeler and Donna "Matilda"
Krewson combine their skills to bring love and laughter
to audiences. Humor differs according to gender, but
its warmth and vibrancy is availabe to all.

Chapter Six

Humor, Morals and Dogma

"Isn't this taking humor seriously
a bit too far?"

Chapter 6 deals with the sensitive topics of humor as it relates to morals and religion.

Chapter 6 describes the dark side of humor and comedy. It gives permission to use humor privately where otherwise inappropriate.

Chapter Six

Humor, Morals and Dogma

There are three things that are real — God, human folly and laughter.
The first two are beyond comprehension, so we must do what we can with the third.

– John F. Kennedy

Bad things happen to good people. Tom was in his second year of teaching the fifth grade. It was Wednesday morning in mid-April. The principal called Tom into his office. The superintendent of schools was there. "Tom, two parents report that you "touched" their girls. Tom was devastated. He steadfastly denied any physical connection to the children. The superintendent explained to Tom the consequences to himself and his wife and two children should this situation go public. Tom was advised to resign. There was an opening in another school in a nearby state. The principal of the school was a friend of Toms' principal. Tom resigned, took the teaching post at the other school and moved his family. The family dropped their complaint understanding that Tom would resign and move away from the community. All was going well until in November of the new school year. In November, Toms' wife sent out their family Christmas letter. That's right, some of the letters went to friends back in the old school district. When the parent of the two girls learned where Tom was teaching; they drove down and " spread" the story of how their girls were "molested". Tom committed suicide. After the suicide, the girls admitted that they had made up the story. They explained that they were mad because of receiving a poor report card that April. What is the role of humor in these kinds of situations? There are times that the road to humor starts with pain and anger. There are situations when humor is inappropriate. This chapter attempts to deal with the dichotomy of life's moralistic situations and the part in it that humor can be involved.

For thousands of years we have turned to our belief in a higher spiritual power for solutions to despicable events. As beneficial as humor is when incorporated into our religious beliefs and faith, there are times in life when it seems out of reach even for "Muggins the Clown."

It was nine thirty at night. I received a call from the hospital. The parents of a nine-year-old child, dying of cancer, had decided it was time to take her off the life support systems. She had requested that a clown be with her at the end. At 11:30 P.M., I arrived at the Intensive Care Unit in full face and costume as "Muggins." After a brief introduction to her parents, I sat in a chair beside the heavily sedated little girl. The nurse cradled her limp hand into mine. There was no conversation. Only the colored lights of the life support system heralded the awesome doom. The lights went off and time froze, as if refusing to acknowledge another medical defeat. Out of nowhere, a soft hand rested on my shoulder. "You can let go now," the nurse whispered, "She is gone." I sat in the room with her sobbing parents asking myself, how could a loving and all-powerful God take the life of this innocent child?

Why do bad things happen to good people? I have been perplexed by this problem since being punished as a child for things I did not do wrong. Part of the answer might be in the nature of the question. What is good? What is bad? To some the line between these two extremes might depend upon your position. We all agree that war is bad. But what if you are attacked? Taking a life is bad, but what if the fetus is deformed or the mother is going to die? The answer to these questions is not as clear. Perhaps what is good and bad is a matter of perspective. We know that humor can create new perspectives. Are there times when humor is a positive solution? We know that what we see as good or bad is often based upon culture and experience. It is good to pat the head of a child, but not in some Asian cultures. There, the head is the seat of the soul and is not to be touched by strangers. In most countries, it is a sign of friendliness to call a child by his first name. In some Asian, Batak cultures, only close family members may address each other by first name. Where I live, death is a "bad" thing. In some areas of India, death is a blessing. When we look around us and consider the issue from a global perspective, the idea of bad things happening to good people is somewhat obscure.

We might cry uncontrollably or laugh hysterically at tragedy. We cry at weddings. We laugh hysterically at funerals. Crying and laughing release tension. Perhaps the question, "Why do bad things happen to good people?" is a trick question. If good and bad are value judgments based upon our perspectives of life, then what is good and bad change? In the mid-twentieth century smoking was considered very acceptable. Today we see smoking as medically "bad". Humor is also is a matter of perspective based upon what we perceive as an acceptable mistake. It is bad when someone falls and is injured, but we laugh when a clown falls and picks himself up. What is good, what is bad and what is humor have one common ground. They are all the result of our perceptions. The death of that child was a situation which I could (or would) not accept. The perceived unfairness created frustration. I sought a way to deal with my grief. I chose sorrow and anger. Perhaps I should have prayed. Perhaps I should have turned on the car radio to some music that would have diverted my attention away from my grief. Perhaps I should have analyzed the event creating a professional distance. The choice was mine to make. The choice is going to be yours.

Doctors, nurses, teachers, ministers, morticians and police have in common the reality of dealing with unfair and tragic situations as a part of their professions. They commonly use humor as a device to deal with unpleasant, sorrowful or tragic events in common. These people have developed specified, private and unique humor that you and I might not appreciate as outsiders. But this humor enables them to cope. To us their humor might appear heartless. In reality this humor provides them an opportunity to distance themselves. We depend upon these highly skilled people to carry on with their professional obligations. They must maintain a clear focus on what they need to accomplish. The role of humor is to allow us to see the absurdity and contradiction of events. Humor can help us deal with the harsh realities of tragedy and hardship. Our commitment to humor is to accept this role within reasonable bounds.

When it comes to morals and truth (dogma), we find that not all humor is humorous. This might sound like a contradiction, but what is humorous to one person is grim to another. Ridicule, satire and explicit sex is considered by some to be vile and vulgar. Yet, controversial as it may appear, this "offensive humor" can be just as healing and helpful as less offensive humor. Tom the fifth grade teacher might be alive today had he accepted his situation as being oppressed. It is the oppressed and depressed who most benefit for ridiculing their offenders, spoofing the situation and using precise and unconcealed descriptions of the persons involved. This is the way you can use humor to deal with anger.

Problems with humor develop when you seek to share it with others. My son treated me to a comedy show. The comedian ridiculed members of the audience. The comedian referred to an overweight woman as "lardo." He asked a man if he used Viagra, then ridiculed his response. He pulled volunteers from the audience and placed them in a situation where the audience laughed at the volunteers, rather than with them. My son and others rolled in the aisle with laughter. I sat transfixed with awe that people did not walk out in disgust. Later, I took my son to see a comedian who specialized in political comedy and satire. The comedian demonstrated great philosophical insight and characterized national political figures with insightful wit. My son slept through most of the program. Comedy is in the eyes of the beholder. What is humorous to one person is revolting to another.

Sometimes humor is comprised of serious and grotesque subject matter. This kind of humor is commonly referred to as "Black Humor". Black does not refer to race or culture. Black means dark or morbid humor. Many people object to black humor because they believe it takes away from truth or pain using negative emotions. This kind of humor tries to get the listener to focus on death, imprisonment, disease, war, etc., through shock statements that are presented as humorous. Another purpose of black humor is to use humor to distance ourselves from unpleasant topics such as dysfunctional families, immorality and violence. It is sometimes easier to laugh at tragedy only when we are a safe distance from it. Some presenters of black humor have no intention of having their audience laugh. The intent of their humor is to gain attention, to focus the audience on their truth, their perceptions or their experiences.

Black humor deals with tragic and grotesque subject matter. It also makes fun of our irrational behaviors, meaningless or absurd situations. Elderly George walks every day from his house to the Post Office to pick up his mail. One day a dog runs out barking and nipping at his feet. This happens for several days with the owner not listening to his complaints. So, he fills a small spray bottle with a mixture of water and ammonia. The next day the dog again comes out barking and trying to nip at his feet. George sprays the dog. The dog runs home. The owner comes running out of her house and screams, "What have you done to my dog? He was just playing!" George pauses for a second. Then in a high pitched scream, he yells "I do not want to play!" People look up in astonishment. Others started to laugh. The owners' face turns red and she runs back into the house. The word "play" caused the humor. George so embarrassed the woman that her dog ended up becoming a gift to the owners' niece who lived in the rural countryside. Sometimes black humor is employed in solving problems or used simply to release ourselves from responsibility. We can enjoy black humor when it does not harm and when it isn't taken seriously. For example, "Ma, Can I play with grandma?" Mother responds, "No, you dug her up twice already this week." How about this one, "Ma, I don't want to go overseas." Response: "Be quiet and keep swimming." Or the T-shirt that reads, "Don't piss me off. I'm running out of places to put the bodies."

The TV series, Roseanne, frequently used a softer version of black comedy in their comedic dialogue. Roseanne and her family lived in a suburb outside of Chicago. In one episode, the entire family decided to get a night's entertainment by bowling. At the bowling alley, Roseanne says to her husband, "Give each of the kids five bucks." He responds, "Five bucks! What do they each need five bucks for?" She explains patiently, "If you give them each five bucks, they'll hang out at the video games all night, stay out of our hair, and we can have a good time." He stops and thinks a moment, then says, "If we gave them each two hundred, do you think they'd move to Cleveland?" Here, the writers used a gentle sort of black comedy to create humor around the difficulties of parenting.

Black humor is often used to deal with social, economic and political problems where we can not control what is happening. War is such a problem. Yet, we can find humor if we chose to look for it. For example the phrases "Fight for Peace," "A Just War," "Censored Information" or "Friendly War" are contradictory words and ideas that loan themselves perfectly to black humor. "War is a grave issue," "I obey freely" or "I will die to protect my freedom," are word plays embracing ambiguity. Black humor is sometimes found inadvertently, like a slip-up someone makes, and we catch: A letter from a soldier to his wife said, "I love it here. I have a nice view of snow-capped mountains, my own bunker and my own machine gun." A letter from a daughter to her dad at war, "Daddy, you always go to war but you don't bring me anything back as spoils."

Satire and sarcasm is a specific kind of black humor frequently used to deal with problems: "Of course the government must lie to the people, but it is for their own good; trust me." Or, "The separation of the head from the body will solve most medical and political problems." Or how about, "It takes brains to avoid a war and war is inevitable."

Humor that conflicts with our personal idea of what people should do or think is often considered offensive. Relating humor to others means that we should be sensitive to their situation. Private Sam Schwartz had a girlfriend named Sally. He went off to serve his country and returned a year later. A friend informed him that his old girlfriend was looking to have a baby. Later, he met Sally at the market. Her stomach was larger. "When do you expect to deliver?" he asked. "I am not pregnant!" she replied. Sam is now out looking for a new girlfriend. Some black humor plays upon ridiculous behavior. For example, when his 38-

caliber revolver failed to fire at his intended victim during a holdup in Long Beach, California, the robber, James Elliot, did something that can only inspire wonder: he peered down the barrel and tried the trigger again. This time it worked. The concept of a person shooting himself in the head is offensive. As an example of extreme stupidity, it is also humorous. Thus, our opinions about stupidity, and our ideas of what is right and wrong (morality), are in conflict. This conflict creates the humor. If both the stupidity and the crime are not humorous, the story is simply offensive. In another example, a chef at a hotel in Switzerland lost a finger in a meat-cutting machine (offensive). The insurance company, suspecting negligence, sent out an insurance investigator to check out the machine. You guessed it; the insurance man also lost his finger. The chefs' claim was approved. There is a bleak, ridiculousness in this scenario, which contains its own brand of black humor. This kind of humor allows us to distance ourselves from painful situations.

Many people limit what might be considered vulgar and obscene to share with their friends who also appreciate this kind of humor. On the other hand the extremes of black humor are on the printed page, found in many current movies or performed by professional comedians. George Carlin is a successful comic known for his black humor. In one of his gags he says, "I recently heard about a mass murderer who killed seventeen people in three days. They said he was a loner. Well, of course he was. He apparently killed everyone he came in contact with!"

Comedians' use of this kind of material has but one purpose — to produce laughter. Laughter can help us cope with that over which we have no control. Black humor can aide us in recovering from tragic situations. Black humor can also give us inspiration that we are not alone in our perceptions. Black humor can provide us a sense of gratitude that our own reality is not bad or wrong. So, when comedians make us laugh, that laughter provides us with a feeling of relief. That feeling of relief opens the way to celebrate life. The celebration of life focuses on the positive and reminds us of the joy in life. Thus, laughter sets the spirit free and helps us shake our heads clear. When we access humor, we experience peace of mind and this gives us courage to carry on. Life will go on in spite of over-whelming loss or discouragement. Why not use laughter to provide relief and empower us to cope?

Black humor can be an important coping mechanism. One example of the current use of black humor is in a recent movie where, in the opening scene, two adolescent sons are asphyxiating their mother as she lays debilitated in bed. The scene was comedic. In spite of its horror, or perhaps because of it, the audience was laughing. Later, we learn the mother was dying of cancer and had insisted that her sons help end her suffering. In this movie, the use of black humor allowed the audience to distance themselves from a series of tragic events in the characters' lives.

Where's Your Humor?

We spend millions of dollars accessing humor by purchasing videos, watching television, reading humorous literature and viewing live performing artists that some people consider vile, vulgar and contemptuous. How we spend our money advertises our commercial support. You can see how accepting we are of different kinds of humor by looking at where we spend our money. Another measure of humor is our desire to choose our friends and companions based in part on their humor. Each of us has our own tolerance for humor. Each of us is different when it comes to sharing our humor with others. The questions are: How does our perception of self relate to how we associate with others? Are we satisfied with these relationships? Can we be better off? How can we find out? The following exercise helps us visually see how we perceive our humor in comparison to our friends and acquaintances. If we are not satisfied, how might we want to change?

Step 1: Setting up the exercise:

Start by drawing a large square on a piece of paper. This square represents all possibilities. Now divide the square into four equal parts. Label the upper left square "A: Friends/Humorous," the upper right square "B: Associates/Humorous," the lower left "C: Friends/No Humor" and the lower right "D: Associates/No Humor."

Box "A" represents friends and close ones whom you feel use "good humor." These are people whose company you really enjoy. You find similar things funny and there is an ease of companionship.

Box "B" consists of those persons with whom you associate, but feel they have a sense of humor incompatible with your own (what they think is funny seldom makes you laugh). You may even find their humor offensive. You do not feel close to these people.

Box "C" are those whom are friends, but you do not consider them humorous. You like them and feel close, but they don't exhibit much of a sense of humor or their humor is different from your own.

Box "D" are acquaintances, people with whom you associate and who have not expressed much in the way of humor with you. These are people you consider more serious in nature.

Your square should look something like this:

A Friends, Humorous	B Acquaintances, Humorous
C Friends, No Humor	D Acquaintances, No Humor

Step 2: Identifying people

Inside one of these squares, put a dot in pencil where you think you fit. If you see yourself as being humorous, and people compliment you on your humor, put your dot high up in box A. If you see yourself as humorous, but others don't always catch the humor, put your dot lower in box A. The stronger you feel is your sense of humor determines how high or low in box A you place your dot. If you don't feel you have much of a sense of humor; if people have commented on your soberness, place your dot somewhere in square C. Base your decision on general perception. You can change your mind later on.

On a separate piece of paper, create two lists. Column 1 is a list of between 10 and 20 individuals whom you consider your fiends. Column 2 is a list of between 10 and 20 persons with whom you have contact, but you have a formal or impersonal relationship with them. Place odd numbers for your friends and even numbers for acquaintances. Your list should look like this:

FRIENDS   ACQUAINTANCES
1. George Brown   2. Ellen Brown
3. Susan Briggs   4. Allan Pynn
5. David Harcourt   6. Sam White

In the above sample list, George Brown is a good friend, but you are not close with his wife, Ellen. Susan Briggs is also a friend, while Allan Pynn is simply a co-worker whom you don't know that well. David Harcourt is a friend and Sam White is someone whom you know simply because he belongs to your club.

Step 3: Assigning "value" to your list of people

Going back to your list, assign a box letter that best describes how you perceive their character. For example, George Brown is very funny and a close friend, so you assign him to "A." Ellen, his wife, is not very friendly with you, but has a good sense of humor, so you assign her to "B." Susan is a good friend but not very humorous — so you assign her to "C." Allan Pynn is a coworker who is fine to work with, but has shared no humor with you, so you assign him the letter "D." David Harcourt is also a friend and has a good sense of humor, but not as humorous as George. You also assign him an "A." Sam is a member of your club and that is the only reason you associate with him. You give him a "D."

Step 4: Placing the assigned values into the square

Going back to your square with the dot, we are going place your list of friends and acquaintances in the appropriate square (A-D). The stronger your perception, the closer your dot is placed toward the outer edge of the box. For not as strong feelings, place the dot closer to the center of the square. George Brown is A1. He is both a good friend and very funny. You write "A1" in box A in the upper left corner. Ellen Brown is not very friendly, but she is funny. You would write her number, "B2" around the lower right corner of square B. Susan Briggs is a friend, but not very funny. So, you put "C3" in the upper left section of square C. Allan Pynn, that co-worker who has not exhibited much sense of humor, would be placed as "D4" somewhere on the left upper side of Box D. David Harcourt is a friend with a sense of humor, but not as funny as your friend George. For David, you would place "A5" in the middle left of Box A. Sam White, is the member of your club, not a friend and not funny. You would place his number, "D6" in the lower portion of box D. In this example, your box would look something like this:

A Friends, Humorous
 	
•   (You)
 	
A1
 	
   A5
	B Acquaintances, Humorous
	
	                            B2

C Friends, No Humor
 	
   C3
	D Acquaintances, No Humor
	
	   D4
	
	              D6

Following the above example, take your list and place their values inside your box. Results will vary according to individual perceptions. But, there are some things to look for:

Look at where you placed your "dot." This is how you perceived yourself at the beginning of the exercise. How accurate was this perception? This is a good time to revise this perception.

Look at the results of your placement. Do you see clusters, patterns or grouping? Ask yourself if these clusters are informative. Examples of this would be, more numbers who are clustered towards the center of your square. They indicate that you surround yourself with neutral people, both intimately and casually. Clusters grouped more towards the left side of box A suggest you have many friends with a good sense of humor. Clusters grouped primarily in Box B would indicate that most of your friends are not very humorous. Clusters in Box D indicate a predominance of acquaintances without a sense of humor, and so on. Make notations based upon your observations.

Look at those placements nearest to your "dot." Is this where you want to be? Say you placed your dot in the box indicating very funny and good friends. In looking things over, perhaps you think you should be more serious. Place a small circle where you want to be and draw a line from your dot to your circle. If you are happy about your placement, how close are you to the other placements? Do you desire to change the relationships between yourself and others in your chart?

Step 5: Changing your placement

There are two ways to change from where you are in order to: 1) become closer to those you want to emulate, and/or, 2) make new friends. Let's say you want to become more humorous. You would identify those friends and acquaintances from your diagram that emulate the qualities you want to learn. Start associating more with them. Observe how they use humor. At home, practice new ideas in the mirror and on close trusted friends. If reasonable, join an organization such as Toastmasters, which will expose you to the qualities you are after. After a while, bring out your diagram and reevaluate your position.

This exercise helps you to see your humor against those with whom you come into contact, without judging yourself as either good or bad. From our first steps, we are taught to be good and not to be bad. In any case, we sometimes confuse making mistakes with being a bad person. Humor enables us to distance ourselves from feeling we are bad and focus on new perceptions. It also helps us perceive mistakes made by others as being simply mistakes, rather than seeing them as being a "bad" person, due to their mistakes.

Humor in Religion

Religion (the belief in a divine or super power) has supplied endless jokes and the source of much of our humor. Perhaps the reason is that there is a lot of contradiction within and between religious groups. A Sunday school teacher was preparing her students to go into the adjoining church for services. As they assembled she asked, "Why is it necessary to be quiet in church, children?" To which one of her students replied, "Because people are sleeping." Most of us are taught that you demonstrate your love for God through respect. We are supposed to take the word of God seriously. Grace and salvation are attainable through good works, discipline and devotion. Is there room for humor? Humor describing our religious shortcomings is acceptable to most people. *"Jack was coming out of church one day and, as usual, the preacher was standing at the door shaking hands. He grabbed Jack by the hand and pulled him aside. The preacher told him, "You need to join the army of the Lord." Jack replied, "I'm already in the army of the Lord, pastor." The preacher asked, "Then how come I don't see you except at Christmas and Easter?" Jack whispered back, "I'm in the secret service."*

There is much debate about the role of humor in Biblical scripture. Many denominations attempt to keep humor and religion as far apart as possible. Yet, there is evidence that humor is an inherent part of being human and being true to God's creation. Think of Abraham. In Genesis, God told Abraham that he and his elderly wife, Sarah, would soon have a son. Abraham must have thought the idea was humorous. How can a man 100 years old, and his wife who is 90 years old, have a child? When they had a child, they named him Isaac, which means laughter.

Faith, on the other hand, is an unquestioning belief. Within most religious faiths, the appropriateness of humor is defined in a simple manner. If the humor contributes to the understanding and acceptance of faith, it is good. If the humor diverts us away from faith development, it is bad. There is little middle ground; you support the concept of humor in the church or you don't. *A preacher ran into one of his parishioners in town whom he hadn't seen at services in quite a while. "How come I never see you in church anymore, Morris?" he asked. Morris replied, "There are just too many hypocrites in church, Reverend." "Well, don't worry, Morris," the preacher said, patting Morris' shoulder, "There's always room for one more."* In this example humor sends a message of Gods' everlasting love and acceptance. *"I heard that new Episcopal Church is so liberal it has six commandments and four suggestions."* This is sarcastic humor that makes fun of a religious denomination.

All religions must deal with the perceived contradiction of taking their faith seriously while at the same time visualizing humor in the both the scripture and the way they practice their faith. No where does this become truer than in the application of clown humor. In 2002, I attended the Association of Presbyterian Church Educators in Toronto, Canada. Some 800 educators from throughout the United States and Canada attended this convention. As a church educator, I attended dressed as a clown. I wore a large button that said "Clown Ministry." During the convention, I interviewed several delegates, representing all areas of the country, concerning how they were involving clowns in Christian education. Their response was generally the same. Their churches knew of clowns. Many had clowns as members of their congregations. Few involved clowns. The reason they gave was that they felt the presence of a clown in their sanctuary would compromise the integrity of the service. They said they would use clowns in their education classes if they were guaranteed that the clown would not confuse Jesus' raising of Lazarus from the dead with "clown magic." After the convention was over, I wrote two articles. In one article, I shared my findings and outlined a generic step-by-step program to encourage religious organizations to involve clowns in faith development. That article was printed in Clown of America International. I submitted a similar article to the Association of Presbyterian Educators, which provided a step-by-step program to safely involve clowns in their church. That article was politely rejected.

"Give Satan an inch and he'll be a ruler." When we take our beliefs and ourselves with such absolute serious-ness, it might become dangerous. Some religious leaders are aware of this and incorporate humor in their sermons to introduce the quality of joy in the celebration of faith. Much of this humor is connected to perceptions from our daily experiences. "Why was Isaac 12 years old when God called Abraham to sacrifice him?" Answer; "because if he had been a teenager it would not have been a sacrifice." Many Sunday school teachers encourage mirth and laughter. One Sunday school teacher asked her Junior High class. "Do you think Moses led the Israelites through the desert for 40 years because God was testing him; or because God wanted Moses to really appreciate the Promised Land; or because Moses refused to ask for directions?" Naturally, all of this is within limitations. Religious leaders must be sensitive to the needs and biases of their congregations. Most church educators restrict their humor to games and general conversation that supports faith development. Naturally, as a clown, I heartily endorse this. After all, one of the first commands given to humans in Christian scripture is "Go forth and make a joyful noise."

Many religious institutions are experiencing reduced membership. There are many reasons for this. Membership in religious institutions is highest during the time of war, epidemics or other long term disasters. We are now not experiencing devastating problems on a national level. One way to encourage membership is to incorporate humor in sermons. Many people today want more than absolution from guilt. People are asking, where is the joy, the humor or the celebration? There is nothing like a clown when it comes to encouraging joy, humor and celebration. The very sight of a clown says it's all right to celebrate your religious beliefs with a light heart.

Humor can be used in religious organizations to help us deal with contradiction and paradox. Joey is a nine-year old boy who attends Sunday school. One day, his mother asked him what he was learning there. "Well, Mom," he began, "Our teacher told us how God sent Moses behind enemy lines on a rescue mission to lead the Israelites out of Egypt. When he got to the Red Sea, he had his engineers build a pontoon bridge and all the people walked safely across. Then he radioed headquarters for reinforcements. They sent bombers to blow up the bridge and all the Israelites were saved." "Is that really what your teacher taught you, Joey?" his mother asked. "Well, not exactly," Joey said, looking down and shuffling his feet, "But if I told it the way the teacher did, you'd never believe it."

The contradiction is between how we want God to view our life and how we actually experience reality. We might put a high value on money while our faith teaches us to put God ahead of money. *A man asked God, "How long is a million years to you?" God said, "A million years is like a minute." Then the man asked God, "How much is a million dollars to you?" God answered, "A million dollars to me is like a penny." The man thought about this for a moment, and then asked, "God, can I have a penny?" God cheerfully replied, "Sure, just a minute."* Subtle, but the humor *makes the point without reprimand or reproach.*

A zealous Christian who was trying to convert a Hindu found himself getting nowhere. "The thing is," argued the frustrated Christian, "You must be born again!" "But, I have been born again!" insisted the Hindu. "And again and again and again." Sometimes issues arise around the comparison of different religions and debate over which is better. *A priest, a minister and a rabbi were all sitting at a table, finishing dinner and talking theology. Suddenly, an Angel appeared before them and said, "I have been sent to grant each of you one wish. Who will go first?" The Catholic priest stood up and said, "I wish for the destruction of all Protestants!" Then the Protestant minister bolted up and said, "I wish for the destruction of all Catholics!" The rabbi remained seated and silent. The angel asked him, "How about you? What do you wish for, rabbi?" The rabbi answered, "Well, if you are going to grant their wishes first, I'll settle for a good cup of coffee."*

There are everyday situations where humor is very effective. You can use humor like a parable to make a point memorable. *A woman invited some people to dinner. At the table, she turned to her six-year-old daughter and said, "Would you like to say the blessing?" "I don't know what to say," the child replied. "Just say what you hear Mommy say," the mother said. The child bowed her head and said,*

"Dear Lord, why on earth did I invite all these people for dinner?" The point of this story is not to rely on the uninformed and untrained to carry on a task you could do just as well or better.

Frederick Buechner wrote: "Is it possible, I wonder, to say that it is only when you hear the Gospel as a wild and marvelous joke that you really hear it at all? Heard as anything else, the Gospel is the church's thing. Heard as a joke — high and unbidden and ringing with laughter — it can only be God's thing." Humor within religion allows us to joyfully embrace our faith, break down barriers and gives us new perspectives. *A Sunday school teacher asked her students to draw a picture of Jesus' family. After collecting the drawings, she noticed that one little boy's drawing depicted an airplane with four heads sticking out of the windows. "I see you drew three heads to show Joseph, Mary and Jesus," she said to the boy. "But, who does the fourth head belong to?" The boy replied, "That's Pontius — the pilot."*

A Sunday school teacher was carefully explaining the story of Elijah the Prophet and the false prophets of Baal. She explained to her class how Elijah built the altar, put wood upon it, cut a steer in pieces and laid it upon the altar. She related how, in the biblical story, Elijah then commanded the people of God to fill four barrels of water and pour it over the altar, having them do this four times. "Now," said the teacher, "can anyone in the class tell me why the Lord would have Elijah pour water over the steer on the altar?" A little girl in the back raised her hand with great enthusiasm. "To make the gravy," came her enthusiastic reply. Humor enables us to make fun of ourselves without loss of self-esteem.

At a gathering of Catholics, a priest was using holy water during a blessing. *A child tugged on his robes and asked, "Father, how do you make holy water?" To which the priest replied, "I boil the hell out of it."* This play on words excuses the inability of the priest to stop and deal with the child's question. Instead, the priest used a pun to set the situation aside.

When you are directly involved in bringing humor, joy and laughter as an aide in faith development you experience a deeply rewarding experience. Clowns particularly enjoy accessing all kinds of rewards in bringing humor and comedy into faith development. Below are some tips to help you successfully initiate and manage becoming a clown, a puppeteer, a magician or a storyteller within any religious organization.

• Education. Be aware of what your ministry offers. Have your mission statement available. If you don't have a mission statement — develop one.

• Set up an Appointment with the Staff. Be prepared to listen. Find out their concerns. Find out what they expect from your program. Have references. Invite comments and criticisms. Leave them with well-prepared information. Ask them if you may call back.

• Develop a Follow-Up Visit. Offer to be part of a feasibility study or a task group to explore program possibilities. Your objective is to find an entrance point. Perhaps it is their youth education program, a special service or at the social hour. Be prepared to grow from humble beginnings.

• Go For An Evaluation. An informal discussion of perceptions can be very informative. I know it is hard, but do not defend! Listen to what they say. Write down notes. You do not have to agree, but do not argue. Toward the end, summarize with them what you have heard.

• Start with a Trial Program. A temporary program, including evaluation after an agreed period, enables everyone to adjust or terminate the relationship without bad feelings. It is important that you view your program as an adjustable prototype.

You now have your "foot in the door." With any luck, your program of humor will bring the joy of faith development into fruition.

People of faith sometimes find themselves faced with potentially embarrassing or confrontational situations. *A minister was on a train when a drunk staggered down the aisle and plopped down in the seat across from him, unaware that he was sitting across from a preacher. The drunk stammered, "I know you. Now, where in Hell have I met you?" The preacher replied, "I don't know. What part of Hell are you from?"* A small insertion of sarcastic humor distanced the offensive drunk and used humor to protect the pastor from potential embarrassment.

Humor can play a vital role when it comes to our morals and dogma. Being an informed humorist can teach you to use Black humor to distance yourself from fear, pain and anger when dealing with life scenarios and situations that are difficult to examine or bear. Black humor is accepted or rejected, based on existing beliefs and preferences of each individual. Our attitudes about what is right and wrong or good and bad, are based on nothing more than our perceptions, our upbringing and the society in which we live. Although we tend to cling to our own definition of "truth," the fact remains that "truth" is subjective and changes from one person to another and from one culture to another. Humor creates a safe bridge between these differences.

Most religious beliefs entail the promotion and development of acceptance and love. We have learned that the power of humor provides us with an enhanced ability to deal with these emotions. Humor helps us gracefully accept those whose faith, cultural beliefs and values contradict our own. Humor helps us "love our neighbors." Humor can serve to bring reconciliation between persons holding different ideas and can lead to change as we laugh at ourselves or our ideas. In addition, the ability to apply laughter and humor to our own faith fosters a light heart. Let's face it; a light heart is more capable of sharing and experiencing love.

Forrest "Muggins" Wheeler delivers chuckles and giggles to children.

Doodle Here

Summary:

Being an informed humorist can teach you to use good humor and bad humor to distance yourself from fear, pain and anger when dealing with life situations difficult to bear. Humor is accepted or rejected, based on existing beliefs and preferences of each individual. Our upbringing and the society in which we live dictate our perceptions. We are all prisoners of our time and culture. Humor enables us to access new perceptions. New perceptions are windows to see beyond the contradictions and ambiguity that might otherwise control our lives.

Although we tend to cling to our own definition of "truth," the fact remains that "truth" is subjective and changes from one person to another and from one culture to another. Humor creates a safe bridge between these differences.

Most religious beliefs include the promotion and development of acceptance and love. We have learned that the power of humor provides us with an enhanced ability to deal with these emotions. Humor helps us gracefully accept those whose faith, cultural beliefs and values contradict our own. Humor helps us "love our neighbors." Humor can serve to bring reconciliation between people who hold different ideas; it can lead to change as we laugh at ourselves and even at our own ideas. In addition, the ability to apply laughter and humor to our own faith fosters a light heart. And, let's face it; a light heart is more capable of sharing and experiencing love.

Doodle Here

About the Author

Forrest Wheeler graduated from the University of Oregon with a Masters degree in Education Administration. He worked with the Portland Oregon School District on its Model School Development Committee and designed American Youth Education Systems. During this time, he also developed models for incorporating humor in the education of children. He spent ten years in Singapore with the Harvard-Lexington (Individually Guided Education Program) working with the British-American Joint Consulate Schools.

After retirement in 1996, Mr. Wheeler began working as a professional clown in which capacity he has won international awards and recognition. In 2000, he founded Clown Interactive Programs, an organization dedicated to promoting the contributions of clowns to communities.

He has published several articles on clowning and tours internationally lecturing on humor in education and the art of clowning. In June 2002, he helped to successfully deliver and protect emergency humanitarian supplies sponsored by the Patch Adams Foundation, *Gesundheit*, to dangerous war-torn Afghanistan armed with nothing more threatening than a red rubber nose.

To Contact the Author For:

Keynotes
Workshops
Seminars
One on Ones
How to start a humor club

CIP
522 Adair, Suite A
Cornelius, Oregon 97113
Phone: 503-992-1329
Fax: 503-429-7050
E-mail: CIP4@msn.com
Website: http//ca.geocities.com/forrest2w

To order additional copies of

Using the Power of Humor

Book: $15.00   Shipping/Handling: $3.50

Book Publishers Network
P.O. Box 2256
Bothell, Washington 98041
Phone: 425-483-3040
E-mail: sherynhara@earthlink.net

Also available at:
amazon.com
barnes&noble.com

All proceeds of this book are donated to C.I.P.
a nonprofit organization to promote humor.